Bring me Sunshine

Alistair McGuinness

Published by Alistair McGuinness, 2023.

BRING ME SUNSHINE

First edition. August 1, 2023.

Written by Alistair McGuinness.

My Hometown

"But that is the thing about Australia, of course–that it is packed with unappreciated wonders."
– Bill Bryson

While writing this opening chapter, I'm enjoying a cold beer in a waterfront bar called The Lucky Shag, surrounded by clientele lapping up the last of the sunshine while seated on decking overlooking the Swan River. It's a mixed crowd for a Friday evening, including a handful of city workers farewelling a colleague, with fun tales to share about her days at the office.

Nearby is a quieter group, seated around a table, while enjoying a different type of conversation. They are studying leaflets and maps and the talk is upbeat, about selfies with quokkas, the balmy weather, the recent sighting of a dolphin and the chance to sign up for an all-inclusive winery tour.

I've ordered Nasi Goreng but am not in a hurry and spend the time watching wispy clouds turn from pink to red, as the sky darkens and the heat of the day refuses to budge. I'm seated a stone's throw from a heritage listed boathouse belonging to the West Australian Rowing Club (Established 1868). Built in 1905, the only remaining two-storey timber clad building on the Swan River looks in pristine condition, painted a creamy white with a large launching deck standing proud above the water. The boathouse is shuttered for the evening before coming to life at dawn, when rowers take to the water in preparation for race day.

I'm in the city of Perth as a weekend visitor and will also be on the move at dawn, not to row along the Swan, but to stroll through the city centre, watching it wake, as café owners open shutters, night shifters traipse home and joggers stride past in search of an unseen finish line.

After living in Australia for 20 years, I still rise early most mornings, no matter the season or the location, from the tropical north to the temperate south. I enjoy being a tourist and occasionally work as a tour guide, taking visitors on trips around the southwest of Australia–once voted as the number one travel destination in the Asian-Pacific Region by the Lonely Planet.

I haven't always lived in the kind of place you read about in the Lonely Planet. I grew up in an industrious, working-class English town, famed for its spirited football team and passionate supporters. During my childhood, there was no demand in town for a tourist information bureau, except for a few flyers in the main library promoting heritage listed buildings within easy reach. One of the most significant is Luton Hoo, an English mansion on the outskirts of town, which has been the backdrop for many period TV dramas and a setting for the romantic comedy, Four Weddings and a Funeral. It is now a five-star luxury spa hotel, with 228 bedrooms overlooking rolling hills, woodland and manicured gardens.

In contrast, my family home had three cramped bedrooms and one bathroom, just like thousands of others in the surrounding estates, all belonging to the local council. During the summer months, I'd team up with teenage friends for long cycle rides into the countryside, with little thought about where we were going or when we'd get back. Along the way, we'd stop for snacks alongside village ponds, sharing our sandwiches with the ducks. Other times we'd make dens in woodland, or push our bikes up steep hills, just for the thrill of tearing down them soon after, hoping our brakes would work before reaching the bottom!

During winter evenings, we'd sometimes skip homework for the chance to play in the damp and darkened streets before bedtime. We'd wear dark clothes and pretend to be on scouting missions while hopping over backyard fences, from one garden to another. Dogs occasionally gave chase and at other times we'd hide in the shadows if ever a back light came on. We rarely made it far, usually because of rain, an injury or frozen terror if a neighbour appeared at their back door, calling out the words we dreaded to hear. 'I know you're out there. Wait till I tell your mum!'

When not roaming the alleyways and streets for entertainment, I'd gaze from my bedroom window at the faraway lights of the control tower at Luton Airport, watching planes head into the clouds. During those moments, I'd daydream about leaving behind suburbia, for the chance to travel far and wide. I also collected travel posters, depicting steamy jungles, snow-capped mountains and tropical islands, with alluring taglines tempting me to pack my bags and lead a life of adventure.

Throughout my happy-go-lucky, free-range childhood, I realised there were two groups of visitors to Luton. The loudest belonged to opposing football fans converging on the town centre during match days. They came from near and far, usually by train and would be guided by police towards the cosy and compact ground at Kenilworth Road, sandwiched between rows of terraced housing, with a rich history dating back to 1905.

The other visitors were greater in number and far quieter, unless making a fuss at the check-in desks at Luton Airport. This demographic would only stay in my hometown for a few hours, spending their time in the departure lounge while enjoying drinks and nibbles. Very few made the effort to explore the town centre before their flight, possibly because it resembled many others in England, with too many cars and people, jammed into narrow streets. Growing up in a town where most visitors seemed keen to leave within hours of arrival, may be the reason I decided at an early age to live somewhere else.

During my twenties, I could have moved to Spain, Greece, or any of the sun-drenched islands in the Mediterranean Sea. Instead, I set my sights on a country I knew little about, apart from mesmerising TV adverts about holidaying in Australia and the chance to get up close to wonderful looking creatures such as kangaroos, quokkas and koalas! In comparison, the only wildlife in my neighbourhood seemed to be stray dogs and alley cats, barking and screeching as passing drunks sang to the stars.

Fast forward many years and Australia is now my home, along with my wife, Fran, and our two children. The journey from England to Australia has been a topsy-turvy one, with twists and turns along the way. These earlier escapades are captured in my adventure travel memoir, *A Taste of Australia* and the journey continues, with *Bring me Sunshine*, offering bite-sized travel stories from coast to coast, including time in the wilds with an Aboriginal guide, followed by close encounters with dolphins, sharks and kangaroos.

This book can be enjoyed as a standalone or as a follow up to *A Taste of Australia,* where the stories came about after a life-changing moment, similar to the 90s movie, *Sliding Doors*. I'll try to explain if you missed out on the film. The fictional plot depicts a person's life taking divergent paths, based upon the result of either missing, or catching, their commuter train.

During the movie, two parallel storylines play out, both wildly different. In one scene, the central character rushes along the platform and just makes their train, leading to a gut-wrenching incident within hours. In the other scene, the doors close just as they reach the same train, leaving them stranded on the platform, which sets in motion a series of events that positively change the course of their life.

The film was so popular that it coined the phrase, *a sliding doors moment,* where an inconsequential incident alters the trajectory of future events.

I hope this analogy gives an insight into the way I felt many years ago, listening to my father-in-law spill the beans during a phone call that my employer was headline news on midday TV. I soon learned that General Motors had unexpectedly decided to close the gates to their car manufacturing facility in Luton, England, with thousands of workers set to lose their jobs.

During the space of that phone call, at the age of 36, I felt my heart racing, knowing that I'd reached a crossroads in my life. This was my *sliding doors moment*–with the option to stay in my hometown and work at the neighbouring car plant or take a payout and live the life I'd dreamed about since childhood–to explore jungles, climb mountains and travel to faraway places such as the Australian outback.

After the news broke about the impending factory closure, I went in search of books and movies about Australia. First, I sat through three comedy classics depicting the antics of a colourful character known as Crocodile Dundee, who lived in a place called Walkabout Creek!

Later, I turned my attention to a cinematic classic called *Walkabout*. This poignant film portrays two city-bred children lost in the outback after being abandoned. Luckily, they were saved by an adolescent Aboriginal wandering the bush to test his survival skills. Throughout the movie, I learned about the unforgiving and untamed world in which he lived as a hunter and gatherer, foraging for food, stalking game and adjusting to the extremes of blazing sunshine and shivery nights in the desert.

In contrast, I'd grown up in a sprawling cosmopolitan town close to London and had never once hunted for my dinner! With dreams of one day exploring the outback and going walkabout with an Aboriginal, I posed the idea to Fran. Luckily, she'd been there during her twenties and had loved every moment. She was keen to return and soon began reminiscing about her time as a jillaroo, working on a sheep farm in the heat and dust of the outback, fixing fences and rounding up sheep. I also learnt that she'd once worked as a nanny in the beachside suburbs of Sydney, with tales to tell about each memorable experience.

We were both approaching middle age and felt the moment was right for a global adventure, although leaving behind close friends and family, especially aging parents, became harder to grasp as our departure date drew nearer. As our plans took shape, I kept thinking about the wildlife we'd encounter in Australia. While in Sydney, would we have to check under every toilet seat, in search of the deadly funnel-web spider? Was it safe to swim in the ocean without being attacked or stung by venomous sea creatures? Would we be able to survive in such a vast country, with no network of friends or family to help us in the early days?

While mulling over these questions, the factory where I'd worked for 13 years finally closed and with the payout I went shopping with Fran for essentials such as rucksacks, sleeping bags and walking boots. We then booked tickets for a worldwide adventure, waved goodbye to family and friends and travelled to Heathrow Airport for the long-haul flight to Quito. While in South America, we volunteered on a conservation project in the Amazon, trekked the Inca Trail and went in search of the final resting place of two Wild West outlaws, Butch Cassidy and the Sundance Kid.

Months later, we ventured to Tanzania and after an arduous climb, touched the snows of Kilimanjaro, the highest peak in Africa. After a lazy week on the sands of Zanzibar, we boarded an overland truck to South Africa, which gave us the chance to raft the Zambezi, camp in the Okavango

Delta and stand outside the cramped cell that once imprisoned Nelson Mandela.

After leaving Africa, we arrived on the east coast of Australia, just in time to enjoy the last of summer. In the weeks that followed, we climbed Sydney Harbour Bridge, abseiled in the Blue Mountains, explored Tasmania and drove along lonely outback roads, with few towns or communities to be found amongst the red dirt and spinifex.

In Melbourne we took tram rides, explored museums and wandered along cobbled laneways, stopping for coffee while soaking up the last of the sun. As the weather cooled, we boarded the Indian Pacific, bound for Perth, Western Australia. The three-day rail journey took us across a treeless expanse of semi-desert known as the Nullarbor Plain. It is here that you will find the longest stretch of straight rail track in the world, extending 478 kilometres into the horizon. We stopped once, at an abandoned settlement called Cook, with just flies for company as each passenger stretched their legs and searched for shade.

This book continues a few years after our arrival in Western Australia. After settling in Perth, Fran fell pregnant, resulting in the birth of our first child, Noah. By the time he took his first steps, we began to get itchy feet. Although we'd enjoyed the joys of a long hot summer, we wanted to be closer to nature, where the pace of life is slower. During a trip to the southwest, we discovered a vibrant landscape, home to world-class wineries and towering forests, fringed by a coastline offering gnarly surf breaks and pristine beaches.

The towns in this region are some of the fastest growing in Western Australia, including Margaret River, Dunsborough and Busselton. After spending time in the community, we began dreaming about one day settling close by. But we also had a yearning to explore other parts of Australia and decided to do this in bite-sized travels, from north to south and east to west.

So, pour yourself a cold drink, sit back in a comfy chair or hammock, and delve into the next set of fun-filled stories, as we go in search of sunshine, adventure and a place to call home!

I Walk the Line

"If you hang out with chickens, you're going to cluck and if you hang out with eagles, you're going to fly."
– Steve Maraboli

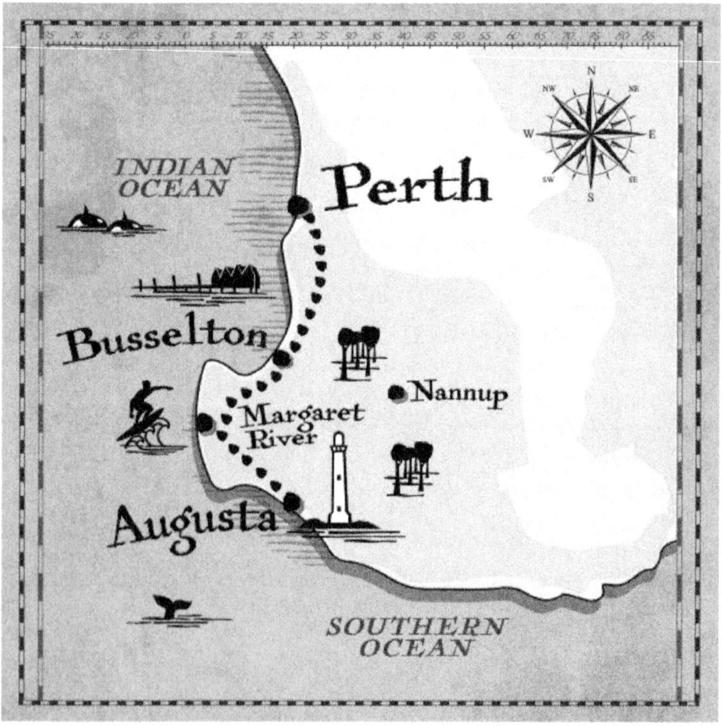

I once got busted for jaywalking in New York city. The ruddy faced policeman had an Irish surname–*O'Malley*–I think, but it was a long time ago. He spoke quickly, just like the yellow taxis racing past to beat the lights. Although I'd timed my brisk walk across the four-lane intersection to coincide with a break in traffic, he was keen to inform me of the risks I'd taken and the rules I'd broken.

I was in midtown Manhattan, within sight of the Empire State Building, hoping to take an elevator to the top. While explaining to Sergeant O'Malley this was my first visit to the USA, I let slip my mum was Irish, hoping that a connection to the Emerald Isle would stop him from reaching for his book. Luckily, a call on his radio cut short our sidewalk chat. Before making haste to something more important, he pointed to a flashing sign above the sidewalk. 'Do me a favour and don't be a wise guy next time. When the sign says *Walk*, that's when you make a move. When it says, *Don't Walk*, just follow the rules, like everybody else.'

And then he was gone, and I was on my way to the Empire State Building with a spring in my step, hoping for a bird's-eye view of the Big Apple, and happy to have met an Irish New York cop!

This incident occurred while I was in my twenties and has stayed with me ever since. Not long after meeting Sergeant O'Malley, I made a pact to say yes to every challenge that came my way. The trigger came after the death of my mum, prompting me to borrow my brother's bike and cycle across the length of Britain with two friends to raise money for a cancer charity.

The 13-day, 900-mile journey gave me the chance to reflect on life, thinking back to special moments with my mum. It also inspired me to take on further challenges, including the chance to climb Kilimanjaro and trek along the Inca Trail. Although I'm not an adrenaline junkie, I've also tried bungee jumping and parachuting. While in Africa, I even signed up to go white-water rafting on the Zambezi. For each heart-stopping endeavour, one attempt was usually enough!

Nowadays, I see myself as a curious traveller, with a passion for hiking and a longing to meet the locals wherever I go. Each time I visit Perth city centre I think back to my encounter with Sergeant O'Malley. He'd be proud of the citizens of Perth, especially the commuters who arrive in the city by train or bus, before walking the busy streets while on their way to work. Most obey the traffic rules, quietly lining up by each intersection while waiting for the signal to cross, as the minutes tick down to a new day at the office. Long after rush hour, when the city streets are whisper quiet, I've watched pedestrians wait for their signal, rather than take a risk and walk across an empty road.

I've often wondered if any of the city workers who diligently follow the road rules while in Perth have ever visited the tall trees in southwest Australia. It is here you'll discover Warren National Park, an area of outstanding beauty spread across 3,000 hectares. Within its boundary you'll find untouched woodland, clean rivers and tranquil camping spots offering the chance of star filled night skies, a world away from the hustle and bustle of suburbia.

Karri trees can grow to 90 metres and those that visit the area get the chance to climb the tallest climbing tree in the world, known as the Dave Evans Bicentennial Tree, which stretches 75 metres into the sky. Compared to the streets of

Perth, there are fewer rules to follow while in the forest. For those looking to climb a tree, common sense and a head for heights are the best attributes when faced with 165 metal pegs protruding from the wide trunk to create a spiral staircase. This leads to a lookout hut 65 metres above the forest floor–or 200 feet if you prefer imperial measurements–but either way, it's a long way to fall.

It is from this vantage point that I begin this story, having clambered up each of the pegs on a solo climb fraught with danger. Before commencing the climb, I'd done my homework–chatting to the barman at the Pemberton Hotel the previous evening while enjoying dinner with my family. The walls of the bar were filled with black and white images of a bygone era, when Pemberton was renowned as a bustling timber town, complete with a mill and hundreds of industrious workers. The mill is now closed and Pemberton has adapted, becoming a popular tourist hub for those who enjoy being close to nature.

The barman was keen to share that no one has ever died falling from one of the climbing trees, although two visitors have reportedly suffered heart attacks after completing the climb! While pouring my beer, he gave a brief lesson about Pemberton and the surrounding communities, which set the seed for me to discover more.

With so many trees in the vicinity, the threat of forest fires during the summer months warrants strict rules and constant vigilance. During the 1930s and 40s, before the introduction of spotter planes, eight karri trees were chosen as fire lookouts and 90 years later, a few of these majestic giants are still climbable. To do so, climbers navigate a series of metal pegs spiralling around each tree trunk. I say *climbers,* but the term is a loose one, as the trees are now a tourist attraction, available to any of those lucky enough to be visiting the southwest. There are no ropes to hold you, or guides on hand to offer support and only one in five climbers reaches the top!

After the thrill of reaching the lookout point, I'm suddenly gripped by fear, not helped by the swaying of the tree as a warm breeze stirs the leaves. I should feel safe, as the lookout hut is cradled between wide branches and held secure by a series of metal struts bolted to sections of the tree.

To capture the moment, I pull out my phone for a selfie and then take a photo of the spiral staircase I've just ascended. Lying flat on the timber deck of the lookout hut, I point my camera towards the forest floor and snap away. Only then do I appreciate the generous gaps between each narrow peg and the wire mesh meant to protect me if I fall backwards during the return climb.

Then I think back to the calming words of the barman the night before. 'You'll be fine, mate. No one's died yet and if you come back tomorrow, I'll pour you a free one.'

With the thought of a celebratory beer waiting for me in Pemberton, I take a breath and get to my feet to admire the view. Far in the distance, the trees thin out, forced into retreat by Yeagarup Dunes, the largest inland dune system in the southern hemisphere. This wide body of sand is ten kilometres long and is forever on the move, blown by sea winds towards the forest at a rate of four metres per year. Reaching 40 metres in places, with steep sides and drop-offs, the dunes are popular for off-road enthusiasts looking for adventure.

Beyond the dunes you'll discover a wild, unforgiving coastline, perfect for those who have the driving skills to navigate soft sand and rutted tracks.

Although alone in the tree, I'm not alone in the forest. Far below, standing in a clearing, is my wife, Fran. She is holding our son, Noah, just eighteen months and blessed with curly blonde hair and a liking for steamed broccoli. I'm convinced I can hear his little voice calling up to me, although any words from so far away are drowned out by the sound of bird life. Moments earlier, I'd spotted a red-tailed black cockatoo, its screeching calls reaching across the forest as it flew above the canopy. It's my time to make a move now, and I vow not to look down. Instead, I'll cling to each of the 165 pegs until my feet touch *terra firma*.

Before my descent on that summer's day, I closed my eyes and breathed in deeply. Here we were, on a family holiday in the southwest of Australia, embracing the fresh air, wildlife, tall trees and sense of space. Within a few days we were due to return to Perth, the city where we'd set up home since moving from England, with plans to explore the country in bite-sized adventures.

After a few years of living in Perth, we had lots to be grateful for. We'd forged new friendships and spent many weekends exploring the outer suburbs, learning more about the city and its people. We'd grown fond of the wooded hills to the east of the city, where residents wait each summer's day for the *Fremantle Doctor* to arrive. Not a real doctor, of course, but a cooling afternoon breeze wafting across suburbia from the coast.

Apart from its urban sprawl, Perth ticks a lot of boxes–not only for its enviable location alongside the Indian Ocean. It is modern, safe and clean, with a network of train lines connecting most suburbs. The locals are friendly and will always give you the time of day if ever you stop to ask for directions. In such a place, where grey skies are rare and enviable beaches are two a penny, you'd be forgiven to think that life is bliss for all that live on the west coast of Australia.

Despite the appeal of Perth, I'd struggled at times with claustrophobia, feeling closed in by its many suburbs. Added to this, I was working for a local business intent on putting profits before people, churning out a range of caravans to meet the growing backlog of orders. Perth was going through a resources boom, fuelled by the demand from China for iron ore and workers were leaving the caravan factory in droves, for the chance of better pay and conditions in the mines.

Although I wasn't drawn to the mines, I knew it was time to leave the caravan factory and had Fran's support. We were also questioning our move to Perth. Although appealing in many ways, we were keen to live somewhere wilder, with open spaces and greenery, along with the chance to live close to the ocean.

With these thoughts mulling in my head, I climbed down to earth, one deliberate step at a time, while holding on tight to each metal rod. At the halfway point, I stopped to take in the scene. The tree trunk was close enough to hug if I dared to let go of the handholds, but the gaps between each one kept me sane as I studied a line of ants marching towards me! Closer inspection also revealed a patchwork of initials, love hearts and illegible words carved into the wood. Most etchings had smoothed over time, either by the elements, foot traffic, or a combination of both. Beyond the army of ants, there were no roads in view or cars rushing past. The only sound was the rustle of leaves and Fran's faraway voice cutting through the serenity, asking why I was taking so long!

A month later, while back home in Perth, I poured two glasses of wine, pulled out a road map of Western Australia and skimmed through the pages. It's the details found in maps I enjoy most of all–the winding roads that few travel on, the quirky or unpronounceable place names and best of all, the chance to venture off the beaten track to experience somewhere new for the first time.

Fran joined me soon after, happy to share that Noah was settled in bed for the night. While sipping our wine, we studied the road map, making note of any nearby places we were yet to visit. We soon discovered there is only one highway heading east from Perth, leading travellers through wooded hills, which finally give way to swathes of rolling farmland before surrendering to the heat and turning into scrub and sand for thousands of kilometres.

We knew all about the road heading southwest, with fond memories of the Margaret River Region, renowned for its wineries, ancient forests, hidden coves and endless beaches. There are no roads heading west of Perth, only shipping channels! Instead, we made plans to head north for a week-long family holiday, to explore nearby coastal communities, with tempting names such as Seabird, Ledge Point and Green Head.

After loading up with water, snacks and luggage, I helped Fran secure Noah into his car seat before turning my attention to the task ahead. There was only one more hurdle to tackle while breaking free of the northern suburbs. Perth is renowned for its many traffic lights and the numbers are fast approaching 1,000 as the city stretches further each year. It's not only traffic signals that appear in each new estate but also fast-food restaurants, drive through bottle shops and shopping centres.

Each time we stopped at a red light, I studied our surroundings and concluded that most new suburbs had a similar layout, including a carbon copy of shopping parades, each with a fuel station, McDonalds, K-Mart and Subway. It felt like Groundhog Day and just as I'd tired of passing another fast-food outlet the road narrowed and the houses dwindled from view, replaced by banners promoting planned developments, all within reach of the Indian Ocean, hidden behind rolling bushland soon to be ripped from the earth.

Close to Perth, the land either side of the road had been put to good use, with fields of ripening crops enjoying a soaking from automated sprinklers. Roadside stalls offered the chance to buy freshly picked oranges, and once or twice I spotted emus in the distance, pecking at the ground. The crops soon gave way to ankle-high stubble and a scattering of rounded hills. Hardy sheep were sighted, standing in the shade of solitary gum trees.

Further on, we passed lonely farmhouses and glimpsed road signs for coastal towns. Compared to the greenery we'd experienced in the Margaret River Region, most of the landscape looked undernourished and in need of rain. There were no wineries on offer, or wooded valleys to tempt us from the comfort of our air-conditioned car.

Instead, we had the Indian Ocean to enjoy, either for fleeting moments in gaps between trees, or for longer periods, when the road ran parallel with sweeping beaches pounded by rollers. Along the way, we stayed at caravan parks offering ocean views and stopped to admire commercial fishing boats, moored close to shore in readiness for their next trip beyond the reef. It seemed to me that every other household owned a boat or dinghy of some kind, but we saw very few people tending gardens or walking the quiet streets.

Each evening before sunset, we'd watch anglers set up on the beach, staking their claim with camping chairs, rods, beers and bait. We also mingled with other campers, each with a tale to tell about their favourite holiday spots. Some places I knew well, such as Uluru, but other locations sparked my curiosity, including the wilds of Kakadu and the marine spectacle of Ningaloo Reef.

With thoughts of exploring such wonderful places in the months and years ahead, we continued with our road trip. Between each settlement, we had the open road to ourselves and spotted livestock behind fences, grazing on bales of hay as the summer sun edged the car thermometer into the 30s. Our final destination was the coastal town of Kalbarri, famed for its laid-back charm. We spent the afternoon pottering amongst tourist shops, before venturing to the beach with ice creams. We were soon rewarded with an aerial display, as three pelicans flew past in tight formation just metres above the water.

After booking into our cabin, we took a sunset stroll into town, to visit one of the local pubs. We had two venues to choose from, each separated by a quiet road and both within sight of the last stretch of the Murchison River, before it turns to greet the Indian Ocean. Although the evening was hot and sticky, the wind had eased, and those within the pub looked happy to be out of the sun. Most patrons were casually dressed–either in T-shirts or singlets, along with shorts and flip-flops. When I say flip-flops, I also mean *thongs*, which is the name that Aussies love to call their favourite summer footwear.

The fish we ate with our chips had been caught locally that day and as Fran and Noah went in search of dessert, I strolled towards a nearby pool table, surrounded by a group of young men. Twenty minutes later I was in action against the winner and potted the black ball while he still had two to go. He laughed off the defeat and introduced me to Davo, the next in line. Australians love to shorten names and places, so it seemed like an easy guess to presume that Davo's actual name was David.

During our game, I discovered he was a passionate fisho (fisherman), who followed Freo each weekend (Fremantle Football Club). Earlier in the evening, he'd been to the bottle-o (drive-through liquor store), in preparation to watch a TV rerun of a game of footy (Australian Rules Football).

I was hoping some of his friends would have similar quick-fire names and they didn't disappoint. Tommo (Thomas) later beat me and then took on Wayno (Wayne). Macca (second name MacIntosh) proved to be a quiet achiever who soon took the lead. His run ended while playing Davo, who made a successful comeback after going outside for smoko (a smoke).

They were a happy-go-lucky bunch, all in their mid-twenties, with sun-bleached hair, permanent smiles and wiry bodies, capable of a hard day's work at sea, pulling in lobster pots. I asked them where they were from and got mixed responses. One or two said they were from 'around here,' and others were from Perth. As for Macca, the tallest of the bunch, he was 'just passing through.'

When not working, they enjoyed off-road trips to isolated beaches, for the chance to fish by day and camp in the dunes by night. When they travelled overseas, the Indonesian island of Bali seemed to be their place of choice, to surf by day and party at night.

After cheery farewells, I left the lads to their game and headed back to Fran and Noah to enjoy one more drink. Darkness had descended by the time we left the pub, but we had streetlights and a crescent moon to guide us back to our cabin. Within a few minutes, the streetlights finished as we came across an expanse of bushland to our left. Moments later, I heard the snapping of twigs and the rustle of leaves. Fran heard it too and held onto my arm, her voice a whisper. 'Ali, what was that? Where's your head torch?'

I kept my voice low, trying to remember where I'd left my torch. 'Don't worry. It's just a possum, or maybe a cat on the prowl.'

The next sound was louder and nearer, made by a wild creature far larger than a cat! Within seconds, a kangaroo hopped into view, followed closely by another. One was as tall as a man and as we watched, they bounded down the centre of the road as if on a date night. They stopped once, to gaze around, and caught sight of us by the side of the road. I thought they'd make a dash for the trees, but they remained perfectly still, watching us with interest, their ears flicking in the pale moonlight.

Seemingly happy, they stayed put for a while, as if contemplating which way to go. Fran squeezed my hand as the seconds rolled past, until, with a flick of their powerful tails, they set off once more down the country road until swallowed up by the night. As we watched them go, I said, 'Well, there's a sight you don't see every day.'

In response, Noah called out from his pusher. 'Mummy, look! Kanga. More please.'

For a few minutes we studied the adjacent trees, hoping for more nocturnal activities, but the forest had returned to silence. Just before we set off again, Fran asked, 'Is this what you're after, Ali?'

'What do you mean?'

'You've always wanted to live somewhere wild and rugged and this place has that feel to it. But there's not much work around, unless you want to join the deckhands for a life at sea.'

She was right about the work front. Apart from those working on boats or in the hospitality sector, there was little else on offer. Later that evening, with Noah tucked up in bed, we spent time on the veranda to enjoy the star-filled sky. With no light pollution to taint the view, we sipped on chilled wine and made bold guesses on the names of faraway constellations.

Despite the clear skies, balmy nights, friendly locals and close encounters with wildlife, the trip away had left us yearning for something more. It was becoming clear that our hearts lay further south, where the air was cooler and the land a little softer under foot.

The following morning, we turned the car around and headed back to Perth. During the drive I said to Fran, 'I'll carry on working at the caravan factory but will keep my eyes open for a job down south. If one comes up, I'll apply.'

'Sounds like a plan,' she said. When I looked over next, her eyes were shut. While Fran and Noah rested, I searched for a tune to play on the music system. While listening to the sound of The Eagles, I drove along the highway, with just the blue sky and red dirt for company. As the fuel dial crept lower, I drummed my fingers on the steering wheel, humming about being on a highway while searching for a sign.

The following Saturday I handed Fran the local newspaper and pointed towards a vacant position listed in the classified section. 'What do you think of that?'

She took a seat and began reading out loud. 'Production Manager required for a thriving business, based in the heart of the southwest. If you have the knowledge and skills to succeed, this could be the job for you. Ideal candidate to have experience in the timber industry.'

After placing the newspaper onto the dining table, she said, 'It sounds promising. Why don't you apply?'

A month later, after a successful interview, we were living in a beachside rental in the seaside town of Busselton. We were just two streets from the calm waters of Geographe Bay, with a friendly neighbour willing to share his catch of fish each weekend.

I spent my weekdays at the furniture factory learning about the people, the processes and the culture. The timber came from managed forests further inland and after a few weeks I took a road trip to visit a few of the mills. Fifteen minutes after leaving Busselton a farmer waved me down, to allow his herd of cows to cross from one field to another, their bloated udders swinging gently as they headed to the milking shed.

The farms soon gave way to protected forest, with tall trees looming close by as the road dipped and curved. Throughout the trip, I spotted crows by the side of the road, pecking at the remains of kangaroos. Then the trees dwindled once more, replaced by farms and smallholdings.

The first timber town I visited was Nannup, famed for its prime location on the banks of the Blackwood River, which measures 300 kilometres from source to sea. It has the acclaim of being Western Australia's longest continually flowing river and meanders through farmland, forests and open plains until passing the riverside town of Augusta, which sits within sight of the Southern Ocean.

After crossing a wide, wooden bridge, I discovered a tree-lined main street, complete with a lush bowling green, historic country pub, weatherboard shopfronts and family-run cafés offering home-cooked delights. After a tour of the nearby mill and the chance to make acquaintances, I then headed to Manjimup, the next town on my list.

Partway through the drive, I noticed a sign for coffee and took the turn. The winding road led me to Donnelly River Village and after parking by an information bay I got out to stretch my legs. The place had the look and feel of a quiet hideaway, with timber cottages dotted alongside a narrow road, each with a veranda and an outlook of tall trees.

While studying the placard and maps on display, I learned the village was close to the Bibbulmun Track, which stretches 1,000 kilometres from Kalamunda in the hills of Perth, to Albany, on the south coast of Western Australia. Considered one of the world's great long-distance walking trails, it is not for the fainthearted, requiring an average time of 50 days to get from one end to the other. Those that take on the challenge encounter towering forests, windswept plains and rugged coastal cliffs, along with the chance to spot a myriad of wild animals and bird life. Nature lovers are spoilt for choice, not only for the peace and isolation but also for the chance to enjoy an area renowned as a biodiversity hotspot, with over 2,000 types of plants and wildflowers found in the region.

Donnelly River Village sits at the halfway point of this epic trail and I watched as two trekkers came into view, each weighed down by backpacks as they stopped by a fallen log to take a rest. While they rummaged in their packs, I stepped inside the aptly named *General Store*, in search of my coffee. The store was filled with all the basics you'd need in such an out-of-the-way place, including the chance to enjoy home-cooked meals, ranging from hearty soups to vegetable lasagne. I also spotted a display of fresh scones and the crumbly remains of a carrot cake, which would go perfectly with my coffee.

There was even a wooden shelf, filled with locally made crafts and produce, including lavender sprays and a selection of honey called Nectar of the Giants. To complete the range there was a dazzling display of wildlife images and stuffed toys, including a cute baby emu called Stripey, made famous by Wendy Binks, an acclaimed artist from Denmark, on the south coast of Western Australia.

While I studied the items on display, it made me wonder how many other creative people were drawn to the south-west of Australia. It seemed to me that it attracted a certain type of person, including the likes of John Tillman, with tales to tell about his time living and working in the forest during the mid-twentieth century. His book, Men and Mill, was on display alongside children's books and guidebooks, some for sale and others to enjoy while sitting peacefully, reading about the people that helped shape the local community.

While waiting by the counter, I picked up a promotional flyer, filled with colourful images of the village and surrounding countryside. The scene looked idyllic, with children sitting by the steps of a cottage, within arm's reach of a juvenile kangaroo that looked cute enough to cuddle! Moments later, a woman entered the store, carrying a box of food while calling out a greeting. 'I hope you haven't been waiting long. Have you booked a cottage?'

I looked up from the brochure and said, 'I'd like to say yes to the cottage, but I'm just passing through. A coffee would be great though, plus a slice of carrot cake.'

While she got to work on the coffee machine, I probed for more information about the secluded village. I soon learned that the cottages were built in the mid-twentieth century to accommodate workers from the nearby timber mill. The mill lasted for 30 years but had to shut when forestry regulations changed. Nowadays, it has heritage status, but is out of bounds because of deterioration. The cottages have fared much better and are available to rent all year round, with many families returning each year.

I also learned that the village intersects with an epic cycling trail known as the Munda Biddi, stretching from the hills of Perth to the coastal city of Albany. The 1,000-kilometre trail carves through a rolling landscape of pastures, native bush and wooded valleys, home to giant trees, wildflowers and rivers.

She served the coffee and cake with a cheery smile and shared a few more snippets about the village. 'It's a magical place which takes you back to nature. Children love the kangaroos, and the emus also get up close. At night the possums come out and there is hardly any noise, apart from the sounds of the forest.'

She then looked around the store and said, 'It's not for everyone, though. There are no big shops nearby and you can forget about Wi-Fi. But if you want to swim in a forest lake, feed wild parrots, or watch a movie in our converted butcher shop, this is the place for you. There's even a 50-metre flying fox, which the children love playing on.'

It sounded blissful and instead of driving off with the takeaway coffee I took a stroll along the quiet pathway. I noted one vehicle parked outside a faraway cottage and a bright green parrot, perched on the branch of a karri tree, watching me with interest. For a while, I sat by the tree to enjoy my coffee and cake, listening to birdsong and the drone of insects. While studying the pamphlet, I discovered each cabin had a wood fire, for use during the cooler months. This would be a perfect getaway, no matter the time of year and as I stood to leave, I noticed a tiny bird foraging close by, with a long tail and bright blue feathers. If it was after a free meal, there was no chance, as I'd devoured every crumb!

With thoughts of purchasing a guidebook on local birds, I continued my journey around the holiday camp, eager to spot more wildlife. During my leisurely stroll, two kangaroos overtook me, as though I was on a city walkway! A few more followed, stopping at intervals to graze on the grass, before continuing their journey through the camp. Moments later I spotted two emus approaching, strutting side by side on the road as if they owned the place!

Just metres from my parked car I caught sight of two kangaroos lazing in the shade of a karri tree. They must have been there when I'd arrived, but my thoughts had been on ordering coffee, not searching for wildlife. They didn't even bother to get up as I walked past. Instead, they gave me a casual sideways glance. Moments later, I was on the road again, thankful for discovering this hidden rustic gem and keen to return with my family.

Within thirty minutes I was in the country town of Manjimup, talking with a yard hand called Phil, while waiting for the mill manager to make an appearance. Phil looked to be in his early fifties, with a thick head of greying hair and ruddy cheeks. He'd worked there for years and knew everything there was about cutting, sawing and grading the locally sourced hardwood.

He was soon sharing his opinion on all things related to timber, including falling quotas, the threat of wildfires in the surrounding forests and the increasing competition from Chinese imports. While we chatted, he pointed to a row of timber cottages by the side of the road. 'They used to be for the mill workers, but some are heritage listed these days. Forestry isn't the same anymore. The old-growth forests are protected and the Greenies want to save all the trees.'

'What's a Greenie?' I asked.

'Oh, you know the type. Tree huggers–hippies–enviro's. They're all the same to me.'

He then set off again, eager to share his point of view regarding effective forestry management. It was clear I had a lot to learn about the pros and cons of logging, including the impacts felt in the community with each new rule and regulation set in place by officials. It seemed to me there was a delicate balance regarding the protection of old-growth forests and the demands for timber products, and I made a pact to learn more.

His final words on the topic were hard to ignore, as he took a trip down memory lane. 'In the good old days, the town used to be buzzing each payday. I remember live music, dancing and a few late nights, but it's a lot quieter nowadays.'

Then out of the blue he said, 'You sound like a Londoner to me. I went there once, years ago, with my wife. It rained most days, with warm beer and too much traffic for my liking.'

After sharing that I was from Luton, a multicultural town, 30 miles north of London, he began spilling a few secrets. 'I bet you didn't know that jarrah from these forests ended up on the streets of London. The wood was chopped into blocks and used instead of cobblestones during the days of horse and cart. It was also used for railway sleepers in parts of the Underground.'

This was news to me, and I was keen to learn more. He then talked about the historic rail network that once connected parts of southwest Australia. Although many sections have been removed or built over, some have been converted to nature trails or cycle paths.

'How long have you been living down here?' he asked.

'Only a few months and I'm still getting to know the area.'

'Well, here's a challenge for you. Try to work out how many towns in the southwest all have names that end in the same two letters.'

'Can you give me a clue?' I asked.

'Yes. You're in one of them now.'

While I mulled over the challenge, he gave me a quick lesson. 'The local Aboriginals are Noongar people and in their language, *Up* means *Place of*.'

It suddenly struck me that I'd recently visited many such places, including Nannup, Yallingup, Dwellingup and Metricup. I made a guess at ten towns and gave him my answer. In response, he said, 'You might be right, as I have no idea! But there are heaps around.'

'What about Manjimup?' I asked. 'What does that mean?'

He held his hands wide in submission. 'I think it means a place of reeds. There are plenty of dams around and the creeks flow well in winter.'

'What about Yallingup?' I asked. 'I went snorkelling on the reef last week and watched the surfers in action.'

He smiled and said, 'You'll need a few dollars to live there, mate. It's a great spot and just inland there are loads of caves. That's how it got its name. Some of the biggest are open to the public, but there are plenty more, hidden away.'

The arrival of the mill manager ended my geography lesson, as Phil slipped away to load a waiting truck. Moments later, I was seated in the main office, discussing the rising price of timber and the demise of the Australian manufacturing industry. Over coffee, I learned it was often cheaper to send Australian timber to China, to be machined into parts, then shipped back for consumers to buy as flat-pack furniture.

Just before I left, he offered some advice. 'You've moved to a lovely part of the world, but the timber industry is on its last legs. If I were you, I'd head to the mines. I hate to say it, but Western Australia's economy seems to be ever reliant on what we dig out of the ground and ship to China.'

As predicted by the mill manager, I soon discovered that the orders at the furniture factory were in gradual decline. As the seasons came and went, the factory limped along. Despite the gloomy outlook, I embraced the changeable weather and decided that Autumn was my favourite time of the year in the southwest. The ocean was still warm enough to swim in, and each visit to the countryside resulted in the chance to enjoy the vibrant colours of the vineyards as the leaves turned red, before bursting into a golden brown.

During this time, Fran's mum and dad made the brave decision to move from England to Australia. Both were in their late seventies and had purchased one-way tickets. After packing their belongings, they said goodbye to friends and neighbours, then headed to Western Australia to live down the road from us in Busselton.

Winter saw the arrival of Sebastian, our ten-pound bouncing baby boy, who entered the world in mid-June, an hour before midday. By the time we celebrated his first birthday, the owner of the furniture factory had put his company up for sale. Once again, I needed to find another job.

While online, I discovered that most local jobs were in the hospitality sector, unless I chose a casual position working in the vineyards. The only vacant position suited to my skills and experience involved working in the poultry industry and the advert looked like this.

Production Supervisor wanted. Do you have the skills and expertise to work in a fast-paced industry? Experience with chicken processing preferred, but all candidates considered. This is a hands-on position, which requires someone with the right attitude and skills to lead by example.

That evening, Fran studied the job advert before asking, 'Is this the kind of job you really want, Ali?'

'Probably not, but there's nothing else out there. If I don't get a decent job soon, we'll have to head back to Perth.'

She didn't reply. Instead, she ambled towards a stack of newspapers due to be recycled. She picked one from the pile, flicked through the pages and pointed towards an advert at the bottom. 'That's from five weeks ago. It looks like the chicken factory has been after a supervisor for some time. Maybe the locals know something we don't.'

'Maybe you're right, but I'm going to give it a go.'

'But you know nothing about chickens, except for the free-range ones we roast each Sunday.'

I already had my answer prepared. 'Chopping up dead chickens and wrapping them in plastic can't be any harder than making cars, outdoor furniture or caravans. It's all about the right flow of materials at the right time. If the systems are in place and the workers are skilled and eager, then life should be a breeze.'

In response, she gave me an encouraging smile. 'I'm sure you'll do a great job and they'll be lucky to have you.'

And that is how I came to be in an interview room with Nigel, the Human Resources Manager from the chicken factory. With his fair hair, youthful complexion, blue eyes and mischievous grin, he looked far removed from the type of recruitment consultant I'd been used to meeting in the past. During the introductions, he requested coffee from the receptionist and offered me a comfortable seat. While waiting for our drinks to arrive, he shared that he'd been at the company for two years, straight from university.

He then sat back and explained the role. 'Alistair, this is a fast-paced environment, with orders going out from midday onwards. We have stretch targets for each product range and your job will be to supervise a production team.'

As the receptionist served our coffee, he continued the spiel. 'Just so we're clear, I won't sugar-coat anything. I see from your resume you have no experience in the poultry industry. Our job is to dissect the dead chickens quickly and safely. We then bag and tag the portions, so they can be distributed locally and interstate. *Fresh is best*, is a saying we love to use. We employ a wide range of people, including some that are on working visas from overseas. Each new day is different to the last and you must be able to think on your feet.'

He then paused for breath before asking, 'How does that sound to you? I haven't put you off, have I?'

In response, I gave him my most confident smile. 'It sounds different to what I'm used to, with rarely a dull moment. Hopefully, I'll be able to put my skills to good use.'

After the interview, he handed me a white gown, along with a pair of gumboots, safety glasses and a hairnet. We then scrubbed our hands before entering the main part of the factory. It was eerily quiet, as he'd timed our visit to coincide with the end of the shift. A cleaner was battling with a knotted hosepipe and as Nigel called out a greeting, I watched a trickle of water turn pink, before spiralling down a nearby drain.

He then led me to an area filled with stainless steel tables, set at waist height. 'This is where most of the filleting is done. It can get frantic at times, and we use contractors to do the job, as they are fast and effective.'

At the end of the tour, he stopped by the exit and turned to face the factory floor. 'So, Alistair, what do you think? Is this the kind of place for you?'

After gazing at the sterile machines, overhead lights, drab walls and concrete floor, I turned my attention back to him. 'I'm sure it will look and feel a lot different when the place is buzzing with workers. Although I'm new to this game, I'm willing to learn.'

His impish grin suddenly reappeared. 'You might find that the culture here is a little different to what you've been used to, but you'll quickly work out who's who in the zoo!'

Just as I was about to enquire further, he thrust out a hand. 'Welcome on board. I think you're the right man for the job and will email you a contract to sign. If all goes well, I'll be here to meet you on your first day.'

Two weeks later, I emerged from my house into a blustery pre-dawn for the 40-minute drive to the chicken factory. Throughout the first part of the journey there were no traffic lights to contend with or roundabouts to navigate, just a country road, partly illuminated by a crescent moon, playing hide and seek between scuttling clouds.

I should have felt appreciative of the peaceful drive and the chance to start a new job, but as I approached the factory gates, my heart began racing. Was it first-day nerves, or something that Nigel had let slip during the interview? The dimly lit car park was empty, and for a fleeting moment I thought that maybe I'd turned up on the wrong day.

The factory was impossible to miss, its weathered exterior illuminated by overhead lights. The floodlit building looked more like a high-security prison block than a place of work, but I dismissed this gloomy thought, took a deep breath and got out of the car. While making my way across the cracked tarmac, I couldn't shake off the feeling that I was walking across a minefield.

Just as I reached the doorway, I noticed someone watching me from inside. Seconds later, I came face to face with Nigel, standing in the flickering light of the entrance hall. He looked dressed to kill, in a white apron, gumboots and a hairnet. As he reached out to shake my hand, his smile looked far too wide for such an early hour. 'It's good to see you again, Alistair. I'm glad the interview and factory tour didn't put you off.'

I wasn't sure how to react, but he changed the topic by pointing to a nearby room. 'Come on, let's get you kitted out before you meet up with Malcolm, the operations manager. He's the man you'll report to from now on.'

While I searched for a pair of suitable boots, Nigel explained how my day would go. 'After meeting with Malcolm, I'll take you through the safety induction. Then I'll arrange for you to meet a few of the leading hands. In a few weeks, you'll meet Oliver. He's the owner and the man that has the final say. Right now, he's about to head over east, with plans to expand the business.'

Soon after, I was chasing after Nigel in a scuffed pair of gumboots as he made haste across the car park, towards a row of portable cabins. The place was filling up fast and I watched as workers rushed past, their heads low against the wind and rain as they made their way towards the factory floor.

Nigel seemed to know most by name and called out to a few as they scurried past. He then waved to a man who was marching from a portable cabin towards the factory. 'Wait up, Malcolm. This is Alistair, the new supervisor.'

Malcolm changed direction mid-stride and bounded towards us within a few steps. While Nigel explained it was my first day, Malcolm loomed over us both, rocking back and forth on his heels. He didn't seem to notice my outstretched hand, as his eyes were elsewhere. I followed his gaze towards the factory and came to attention as he asked, 'Do any of you know how to fix industrial freezers? The new one keeps tripping and the others are crammed full.'

After receiving two blank looks, he quickly left the scene, muttering to himself about the place falling apart. Nigel watched him go and said, 'As you can see, he's a busy man, but we'll hopefully meet him again later. Mind you, I'm glad we don't pay him for the number of steps he takes each day, as he rarely stands still.'

He then steered me towards the rear of the factory, which led into a dimly lit corridor filled with empty crates. With each step the temperature dropped, and in the gloomy surrounds there was little sound, apart from our footsteps on the uneven floor.

The cold seeped through my thin clothes and as I began to shiver, Nigel gave a word of advice. 'No need to wear office clothes, Alistair. This is a frontline job and you'll need a thick jumper and thermals instead of a shirt and trousers. Think of it as working in a giant-sized fridge all day!'

For the next 30 minutes, we wandered throughout the factory, as Nigel pointed out various machines used by the production workers. By the time we'd returned to his office, I'd already called Fran, with an urgent request that she go shopping for thermals. Luckily, his office had a portable heater and as I warmed my hands, he skimmed through a safety induction. Once complete, he said, 'Okay, I think it's time to show you the production office. With a bit of luck, we'll bump into Malcolm along the way.'

We bumped into him–literally! He was charging along a corridor, phone to his ear, barking instructions to whoever was at the other end. While heading past, he waved briefly, with a promise to meet up soon. Moments later, I was standing in a musty room, surrounded by messy desktops, discarded machine parts, toolboxes, cleaning equipment, technical manuals and piles of paperwork. Nigel waved a hand across the room and said, 'This is where you and Malcolm will meet each morning. It needs some TLC, but is close to the production line, which is where you'll be spending most of your time.'

Just then, the door sprung open, and Malcolm marched in while talking on his phone. He headed to a table and began rummaging through each drawer, before turning his attention to a selection of cardboard boxes strewn across the floor. By the third box, he got lucky and pulled out a piece of printed paper. After ending the call, he let out a breath and made his way towards the door. I called out a greeting, which stopped him in his tracks. 'Oh, there you are. I've got a few minutes to spare if you want to know anything.'

My mind whirred with questions, but the first to pop out wasn't the one I'd planned to ask. 'Have you ever considered getting a personal assistant?'

He produced an even smile and gave a straight-faced answer. 'We don't have that luxury here, Alistair. This is a lean, mean, family-run business and we all need to pull our weight.'

I didn't want to upset my new boss on day one and quickly changed the topic. 'I totally agree, Malcolm. Lean and mean sounds exciting. By the way, I'm keen to learn where the production schedules are kept. Will I need a username and password for my computer?'

He took a step nearer and slowly shook his head. 'Just so we're clear. I don't need a computer, and neither will you. There is nothing better than a notebook and an excellent memory. I've been working here for a long time and—'

A sharp knock on the door interrupted him, followed by the sight of a young woman with a concerned look on her face. While peering at us from a safe distance, she said, 'Malcolm, I'm afraid we have a problem with the Adelaide order. It's overdue and the client is after some answers.'

He fled to the door, promising to meet me again during lunch. He never showed up, so after eating alone, I took a walk. While navigating my way along an outer corridor, I heard a crashing sound, followed by someone shouting. I rushed around the corner to find a man on his knees, frantically picking up metal trays strewn across the floor. Although he wore a hairnet, his mass of greying curls looked eager to escape. As he stood, I noticed a pair of tired eyes, studying me with caution.

The trolley he'd been pushing had one of its wheels jammed into a broken drain. I stopped to offer help, but he ignored the gesture and began to rant and rave. 'This place drives me nuts. The trolleys are clapped out, the drains are a dog's breakfast and the broken floor tiles are like crazy paving.'

After calming down, he eyed me suspiciously. 'Who are you then? Are you new?'

'Hi, I'm Alistair. This is my first day on the job.'

'Are you related to any of the managers?'

'Not that I know of. I'm here as the new production supervisor.'

I then asked him his name and stuck out a hand. Although he didn't reveal his name, he shook my hand while sharing his thoughts. 'The last supervisor quit after a few weeks and I reckon you'll be the same–unless you're desperate for the money of course.'

'What are you on about?'

'The factory is a madhouse, I tell you. Have you met Bruce yet? Probably not. He's meant to be the safety manager but rarely leaves his office, except to measure the temperature each day. He wants us to work in a fridge but turns a blind eye to the blocked drains and broken lights. As for the owner, he must be off his rocker! Instead of cruising around the world or playing golf, he spends most of his time spying on us. Have you seen all the surveillance cameras?'

As I shrugged my shoulders, he gestured towards the far end of the corridor and lowered his voice. 'Don't worry mate, as this section is out of view.'

He then dragged the trolley out of the dip, gave the squeaky wheel a kick of disapproval and continued his journey without another word. While walking to my office, I spotted a mounted camera and ducked as it slowly turned towards me.

Once safely inside the office, I decided to give it a spring clean. One cabinet was crammed with marketing pamphlets dating back many years, and the drawers to my desk were filled with an assortment of hand tools, along with nuts, bolts and untouched maintenance manuals. I also discovered a cardboard box filled with reels of stickers, now yellowed with age. The words, *Fresh is Best*, were stamped across each one.

The best find was a box of movie DVDs, which I rummaged through to find any gems. Most were high-octane, low-budget thrillers, but the one at the bottom caught my attention. It was called, *One Flew Over the Cuckoo's Nest.* I pulled up a chair and studied the cover, depicting a rebellious Jack Nicholson, wearing a leather jacket and black woollen hat. While reading the movie description, the memories came flooding back of a time long ago, when I'd sat and watched the film with one of my brothers, Michael.

At the time, he'd lived and worked in London but would show up at the family home each month, with stories to tell and gifts to hand out. Sometimes it would be fashionable T-shirts for his siblings, or something quirky from Camden Town for our mum. He also used to bring along a selection of movie DVDs and would encourage me to watch some of them with him. At first, I resisted, as I was used to watching madcap teenage flicks, not Hollywood classics.

But with perseverance and the right choice of films, he soon opened my eyes to another world. After we'd watched *One Flew Over the Cuckoo's Nest* together, I fell silent as the last scene hit home. Michael then waited a few moments for it all to sink in before asking, 'So, Ali, what did you make of that?'

I remembered wiping away a tear and saying, 'I'm not sure if I'm meant to be laughing or crying. It was very sad, but also kind of funny. I can't stop thinking about the Indian chief and the way he fooled them all.'

'What about the head nurse?' he then asked.

'I didn't like her.'

Michael nodded and said, 'Maybe she needed to run the ward with an iron fist. Was she cruel or smart, or both? There's a moral in the story somewhere. Maybe it's the mental patients that thought they wanted freedom, but soon discovered they couldn't cope in the real world. Or maybe the film is about the choices we make and where they lead us. For the Indian chief, maybe his fear was going back to alcohol if he ever got released into the outside world again. Maybe it's as simple as keeping quiet while waiting for the right moment.'

Although many years had passed since that day, the thoughts we'd shared seemed just as relevant as I sat alone in the production office, pondering my next move. Seconds later, Malcolm burst into the room and noticed me holding the DVD. I asked if I could borrow it and got the nod of approval as he rummaged through a pile of paperwork.

After snatching a piece of paper from the pile, he dashed towards the doorway, calling for me to follow. As we raced along a darkened corridor, he explained that a courier had just arrived to collect an order of frozen chicken breasts for a client in Kalgoorlie. The boxes I needed to find had been stamped with the customer's name, but no one could remember which freezer they'd been put into. Two hours later, with aching arms and frozen toes, I drove out of the car park, after searching through hundreds of ice-cold cartons to find the 20 I needed.

Malcom proved to be elusive during my first week, which meant I had little to do as he rushed around in circles. Each time I offered to help, he dismissed the idea, saying he didn't have the time to explain. He occasionally sent me on errands to find missing stock items and during this time I got to meet and greet many of the production workers. Some were quiet and made little fuss, while others complained about poor pay and the frantic rush to meet each new deadline. Although they seemed like decent, hardworking people, there was no buzz on the factory floor. Instead of background music and banter between fellow workers, the only sound I heard was the rumble of machinery and the swishing of blades.

I soon became fascinated by the work that took place in the narrow corridors between the factory floor and industrial freezers. Workers trudged up and down, pushing clapped-out trolleys piled with boxes of sliced-and-diced chickens. They rarely spoke, apart from those who cursed the bent and buckled trolleys, which seemed to have a life of their own on the uneven floor.

Sadly, the scene reminded me of another classic film I'd watched with Michael, called *Midnight Express*. The movie is based on a true story, about a convicted American drug smuggler called Billy Hayes, who gets sent to a dank and foreboding Turkish prison and finds himself in a ward full of insane inmates.

Some of these deranged prisoners congregated each day to walk in circles around a stone pillar. All of them trudged in the same direction, either chanting or in silence, for hours at a time. One day, in desperation, Billy walked in the opposite direction, which resulted in tussles with some of those he bumped into, as they pleaded for him to turn around. To me, the workers in the corridors of the chicken factory had the same glazed look as they struggled with their antiquated trolleys.

During my explorations, I discovered Jimmy, the maintenance man. He was short and stocky, with a plump belly and tightly curled auburn hair. He'd greeted me with a bone-crunching handshake, followed by a smile and a joke. I soon learned that he was a part-time worker, looking to earn a few dollars to pay for beer money and a bet on the horses. His Irish lilt was impossible to miss, but he seemed reluctant to share which part of the Emerald Isle he was from. I guessed Dublin, which resulted in a shake of the head and a smile, followed by the words, 'Not even near.'

His workshop was housed in a portable cabin, crammed with tools, machine parts, and enough junk to fill a skip. In one corner stood a pedestal drill, alongside a welding machine, kettle, fridge and a tea-stained mug. His parting words during our first meeting gave me the rare chance to smile. 'You can pop over for tea whenever you'd like. If it gets too much in the days ahead, I have a wee bottle of whisky at the ready.'

He then winked and said, 'For medicinal purposes, of course, to keep us all sane!'

Midway through my second week there was an uproar in the boning section, because of a personal dispute between two contract workers. This led to a bloody nose for one person and a cut lip for the other. Friday afternoon proved far more exciting. Partway through the shift, the machine that chopped the heads off each chicken had ground to a halt and wouldn't restart. Within minutes there was a backlog of trussed chickens on the overhead conveyor, their limp and lifeless bodies hanging in the cold air. Malcolm was nowhere to be seen and the nearby workers were running out of chicken parts, so I dashed outside, in search of Jimmy.

His workshop was empty, but I found him nearby, dozing peacefully in the driver's seat of his van. I tapped on the window and watched as he came to life, his green eyes staring through the windscreen. Moments later, he set off towards the factory, screwdriver in hand, muttering to himself about the state of the machines.

While back in my office, I found some scrap paper and wrote a report, including a list of ideas to improve morale, productivity and safety. Just as I'd finished, Nigel appeared at the doorway. 'Hi, Alistair. How's it going? All good, I hope.'

Instead of waiting for my answer, he led me to the lush office belonging to Oliver, the man that ruled the roost. Along the way, he explained that Oliver had just returned from a successful business trip and was keen to hear how I was getting on.

From the moment I set eyes on Oliver, I couldn't stop thinking about his resemblance to a fully grown rooster. He had a wide chest, ruddy face and a full head of slicked-back hair. He didn't stand up as I walked into his office or hold out a hand to greet me. Instead, he gestured to a nearby seat and said, 'So, Alistair, how have you settled in so far?'

I placed the handwritten report on his desk and said, 'The first few weeks have been an eye opener for sure. I'm looking forward to sharing my thoughts with you and Malcolm, so we can help to improve—'

He held up a hand to stop me. 'Don't go worrying yourself with reports. I have managers that can do that sort of thing for me. Your job is to do whatever Malcolm requests. Nothing more and nothing less.'

He then gestured to an overhead screen. 'From this chair, I get to see everything that goes on across the factory. As you'll have worked out by now, the workers always give a hundred percent. We rarely get complaints and always comply with the room temperature regulations for each working space. I hope you aren't one of those people who complains about working in the cold.'

I didn't want to share that my toes were suffering near frostbite, despite the double layer of thermal socks Fran had bought for me after my first day. Instead, I tried to keep the conversation jovial. 'I'm from England and have always enjoyed a frosty morning. Now I have that pleasure every day, rather than a few times a year.'

He muttered an acknowledgement and turned his attention towards the screen, which had scrolled from one camera to another. I caught sight of Jimmy, standing on top of a stepladder while trying to prise a jammed chicken from the conveyor. Malcolm was holding the bottom of the ladder while studying his phone.

Oliver didn't seem to notice and swiftly selected another camera. I recognised the next scene at once. It was one of the cramped and dimly lit corridors, filled with workers in transit, each with an overloaded trolley. To me, it resembled a third-world roadway, with no rules or regulations to get past the broken vehicles or those too slow or overloaded. Oliver let out a hearty chuckle and said, 'Look at that, Alistair. Lots of workers going about their day without a—'

His words were cut short as the next camera came to life. Although there was no sound, it looked to me as though the man in view was laughing loudly, while a nearby colleague told a joke. Together, they were stacking heavy boxes into a freight truck and as I watched, they continued with the task at hand, trading jokes and smiling while they worked.

In response, Oliver reached for his phone and tapped a well-known number. 'Malcolm, I want you to head over to the dispatch area. Tell the two workers that if they want to share jokes with each other, they can join a circus instead of working here.'

He then ended the call and smiled at me once again. 'Well, that sorts out that little problem. I hate foolhardy workers, don't you?'

I realised this man didn't reason too well, so I played dumb. I nodded slightly and feigned an interest in the monitor, which soon had Oliver scrolling through the cameras for something of interest. After satisfying himself that all the other workers were being productive, he rose from his chair and said, 'You can go now, Alistair. By the way, Nigel insists that you're the right man for the job. I do hope he is right!'

By now it was late on a Friday, and Malcolm was still running around the factory. While making a dash for freedom, I heard Nigel calling my name. He ran over, grinning with enthusiasm. 'Alistair, guess what? We need you to run the bagging room on Monday. The team leader has just quit, so you'll be in charge.'

Five minutes later I was standing in the bagging room with Nigel, watching as a cleaner hosed down the walls. Nigel led me to the far corner and explained how it all worked. 'Can you see the hatch in the wall up there? It leads to a machine where we soak the chicken in some type of solution. It might be brine, but I can't be sure. Stewart and Damian run that section and they'll pop their heads through the hatch at six on the dot, to say hello. They'll have a batch of diced chicken ready to hand over.'

He then turned his attention to the largest structure in the room, which looked to me like an oversized pinball machine. It was made from stainless steel, with blood and guts dripping from the framework.

Nigel noticed me staring and said, 'Don't worry about the mess, as the machine is about to be cleaned. By the time you arrive on Monday, it will look brand new.'

I looked around, noting the oversized flippers that propelled chicken pieces into various chutes, depending on information gained from a series of sensors positioned along the sloped table. Production workers would man these and their main task would be to bag the chicken pieces, before storing them in boxes.

While I studied the machine, Nigel gave a running commentary about each part of the process. Although impressed with his knowledge, I still had one more question. 'It looks simple enough, but will I have an experienced crew?'

He gave me that look again, the one that told me everything was not how it should be. 'Well, the good news is that you'll have a team of five. Plus, I've seen the machine in action and will be here to get you going.'

'And what's the bad news?' I asked warily.

'Two of the crew will be brand new. They're flying in from Seoul today, to work on temporary visas.'

'This sounds interesting,' I said.

'Don't look so worried, as Min-soo will be here to help. He's also Korean and will interpret if needed. He's a clever guy and knows this machine like the back of his hand.'

Just before we left, Nigel gave a word of warning. 'This machine is getting old and plays up from time to time, especially on chilly mornings.'

'It's chilly every day, Nigel. So does that mean it will play up for me?'

'I reckon you'll be fine, but I know a few workarounds to keep it going. If the machine plays up, just whack the side with a rubber mallet.'

'Nigel, what are you on about? You can't just whack a machine and hope for the best. Does Jimmy know about this?'

He dropped his voice and mumbled a reply. 'I guess he does, but I'm not sure anymore as each problem seems to blur into the next.'

Then his eyes lit up, followed by a mischievous grin. 'Mind you, it must be fun to let your frustrations out by bashing a piece of clapped-out machinery with a lump of rubber.'

Without waiting to hear my reply, he laughed away the comment, wished me all the best for the weekend and turned his attention towards the cleaner. As I made my way to the car park, our paths crossed again. By now, his slender shoulders had hunched and the usual bounce in his step had been reduced to a weary plod. As he looked up, I said, 'Thanks for all your help, Nigel. Since joining, it's been a real eye opener for me.'

He managed a smile and said, 'No worries. You'll get used to it after a while.'

In the quiet confines, without prying cameras, I had a heart to heart with him. 'Nigel, you seem like a decent bloke, but I've never seen someone from HR get so involved with production and cleaning tasks. Shouldn't you be working on other things, instead? People keep leaving and morale is rock bottom. This isn't normal, you know.'

'I guess you're right, but I've given up on all of that. The other managers don't listen and it's far easier to firefight each day. Maybe I need to escape for a while.'

His words struck home, and I pulled the DVD from my bag. 'Nigel, I found this in the production office and Malcolm said I could borrow it. Have you ever seen it?'

He studied the cover to *One Flew Over the Cuckoo's Nest* and shook his head. 'Your office hasn't been cleaned in years, so the movie could belong to anyone. Is it any good?'

'It's a classic, and I think you'll get a lot from watching it. In some ways, this place seems like the institute in the film. But not all the inmates give up. Some fight to the end and one of them makes a break for freedom.'

He studied the cover again and said, 'I appreciate the offer, but I don't think it's my type of movie. You go ahead and enjoy it.'

After watching him drive off, I made haste, in case Malcolm or Oliver arrived on the scene. While driving home my thoughts turned to Bruce, the reclusive safety manager. With luck, I'd get to meet him within a few days to share my thoughts and observations.

That evening, while sitting with Fran by the firepit, I watched the stars come to life. With the children tucked up in bed, I should have felt relaxed, as Fran poured wine and asked about my day. For a fleeting moment, I pondered sharing a few stories, but didn't want the evening to be ruined.

Instead, I prodded the logs and gazed into the fire, before reaching for a travel supplement from the newspaper. After a few seconds, I found my voice again. 'Fran, I'd rather not talk about chickens just yet. The weather is looking good for the weekend and I'm looking forward to some fresh air and winter sunshine. Do you fancy a mystery tour tomorrow, with me as the guide?'

She raised her glass of wine in acknowledgement and moved closer to the flames. I sipped my drink, flicked through the magazine, and came across a striking image of a lighthouse, positioned on a jut of land. The low-lying hills close by were covered in bushland, with just a narrow coastal road to gain access to the lighthouse. The article was called, *Next Stop–Antarctica.*

I made a note of the directions, closed the magazine, and finished my drink. As I did so, Fran asked, 'Is everything okay? Do you have a plan?'

'Yes,' I said. 'I think we'll have fun tomorrow, with plenty of fresh air and panoramic views to remember.'

*

Our Saturday morning started with a drive to Margaret River, to spend time at the farmer's market, at the southern end of the popular country town. The mood was upbeat, with many stalls offering visitors a wide range of delights, including wood-fired bread, fresh fruit and vegetables, locally made garments and free-range eggs. As Fran and the boys mulled over some savoury delights from a French baker, I sat on a nearby bench, enjoying the winter sun while listening to a busker.

Forty minutes later we were on the narrow approach road to Cape Leeuwin and all eyes were on a bright white lighthouse, taking pride of place on the rocky shoreline. After parking the car, I turned towards Noah and Sebastian. 'Well boys, we're at the most south-westerly point of mainland Australia. What do you think of that?'

Seby studied me from his baby seat and gave a one-toothed smile. Noah pointed towards the distant lighthouse and said, 'Daddy, I need the toilet.'

After paying the entrance fee, we set off along a quiet roadway, passing three cottages built between 1885 and 1886, to accommodate the lighthouse keepers and their families. Their task was to assist with the continual operation of the station, 24 hours a day, every day of the year. The distance between each cottage looked to be 40 metres and each had enviable views of the Southern Ocean from their backyards, with an expanse of grass sloping towards a rocky shoreline.

Another similarity was their high-pitched roofs, designed to defend against ferocious winter storms. After reading a nearby placard, I discovered the two southern residences had been built using local limestone and the third, from granite located close to the lighthouse. I also learned the lighthouse was converted to automatic operation in 1978, signalling the end for full-time keepers. It became the last manned lighthouse on mainland Australia, with the last keeper leaving in 1996.

After passing the cottages, we came to the lighthouse, with the Indian Ocean to our right and the Southern Ocean to our left. While standing by the headland, I was hoping to spot mighty waves pounding against each other at the point where the two oceans converged, but there was no way of knowing where one ended and the other began. It felt like we were standing on the edge of the world, with just the wind for company and a gull in flight, just metres from the choppy waters.

We then turned our attention towards the base of the lighthouse where a handful of visitors waited patiently. A bright-faced man, dressed in a matching pair of khaki trousers and thick jumper, appeared by the doorway and called out, 'The lighthouse tour is about to begin. Please have your tickets ready.'

The children were too young to take the tour and Fran was happy to stay behind. With promises to wave from the top, I handed my ticket over and stood in line with the other visitors. I learned many facts within the first few minutes, including the name of our guide (Paul), the height of the lighthouse (39 metres) and its feat of being the highest of its kind on mainland Australia.

With a cheerful grin, Paul led us inside to begin the tour, which included a climb to the observation deck via a narrow spiral staircase. During the ascent, I counted the number of steps, as Paul gave a history lesson and pointed out pieces of machinery used within the lighthouse. After 176 steps, we stopped to catch our breath, before Paul led us through a narrow doorway onto the viewing balcony. All at once my breath was taken away again–not only by the stiff breeze but also by the bird's-eye view of the wild and rugged headland. We were shielded from the drop by metal railings, which wrapped around the viewing deck to enable each of us to enjoy the 360-degree views.

I spotted Fran and the boys, standing on a grassy bank while waving up at me. I called out a greeting, but they didn't seem to hear a thing! Out to sea, rocky outcrops and small, uninhabited islands could be seen. Some disappeared every few seconds, replaced by waves and white water. Although Paul spoke loud and clear, the wind snatched away some of his words.

'The lighthouse was constructed from local limestone... the original light source was a six-wick kerosene lamp until conversion to electricity in 1982... the lighthouse keepers lived in nearby cottages... supplied with essentials every two months by boat... with wind speeds of up to 130 kilometres... 22 shipwrecks before the lighthouse was built... blue whales have made a comeback and can be seen... homemade soup at the café...'

Before the descent, we were given free time to walk around the observation deck. I completed two circuits before stopping to admire the three cottages, far in the distance. It struck me how isolated the lighthouse keepers would have been from the outside world, their houses perched close to the water's edge, with few creature comforts. Such dedication is rare these days and for a moment I considered the possibility of scooping Fran and the boys up, to travel far and wide to give them a similar experience, far from the TV and technology.

After the tour had finished, I thanked Paul and asked for advice on where to go for a late lunch. He recommended the onsite café or a trip into Augusta for the chance to visit the closest fish and chip shop to Antarctica! This sparked our interest and after waving goodbye we drove down a narrow road overlooking the Southern Ocean, passing houses with enviable views as we made our way to the riverside town of Augusta.

As we approached the outskirts of town, Fran spotted a colourful sign by the side of the road depicting a penguin wearing a chef's hat. An arrow directed us towards the Colourpatch café, offering far-reaching views of the Blackwood River from its vantage point. The waterfront was quiet, with just a few parked cars and a lone fisherman, casting a line from the town jetty. While waiting for our fish and chips to be cooked, I chatted to the girl at the counter.

I soon learned that the riverfront comes alive each spring and summer, especially with families looking to enjoy time away from the city of Perth. With many campgrounds in the vicinity, along with a hotel bar, bakery, shops and cafes, the township seemed like an ideal spot, especially during the holiday season. The arrival of our fish and chips coincided with the spotting of a dolphin, cruising the shallows in search of food.

After waving goodbye to the girl, I joined my family on a grassy bank close to the river's edge and together we searched for dolphins while tucking into hot chips and battered fillets of whiting, caught a day earlier in the Blackwood

River. Far to our right, the Southern Ocean pounded the exposed beach, but our part of the world seemed to be protected from the wind by an expanse of trees overlooking a children's park.

On the far side of the wide river, the land looked untouched, with no signs of civilisation. Instead, it had many trees and bushes, stretching into the distance, resembling a vast, uninhabited wilderness. It seemed to me that Augusta was a special place, just off the beaten track, with a sense of space and bracing fresh air, courtesy of the mighty Southern Ocean.

As the last of the chips were devoured, we watched as a fisherman appeared from upstream, his motorised boat cruising along the river. He wore shorts and a flannel shirt, along with a baseball cap, and waved to the children as he moored by the riverbank. After stepping barefoot into the water, he headed to a nearby filleting table located a few metres from the bank. Noah was soon barefoot in the knee-deep water, watching with interest as the fisherman filleted his catch of herring.

Other guests began arriving at the scene, as three pelicans glided in for a perfect landing, before paddling their way towards the waterside table. They were rewarded with rich pickings, as were the stingrays that appeared without warning and caused a flurry of excitement as Noah leapt from the water. In response, the fisherman called out, 'Don't worry. They won't harm you. They're eagle rays and they visit me most days in search of a few scraps.'

After a moment of hesitation, Fran joined Noah in the shallows while I sat on the grass with Seby and took photos.

The stingrays moved gracefully over the sandy surface, their dark fins rippling as they brushed past three pairs of legs while searching for food.

While Fran drove us home, I skimmed through the weekend newspaper. What caught my attention was the number of articles that mentioned the increasing demand for iron ore from Chinese steel mills. The mines to the north of the state were ramping up production and there was talk of a looming skills shortage.

One article showed two miners from the Margaret River Region, proudly dressed in fluorescent work shirts. They'd recently given up local jobs, for the chance to double their wages by working two weeks on, two weeks off, at a remote mine site, located close to the desert. I also learned that their camp had many facilities, including an outdoor pool, gym, walking track, games room and café.

Compared to the chicken factory, their working conditions sounded ideal, except for being away from home for such long periods. I closed the paper and peered at Noah and Sebastian in the back seats. They'd both fallen asleep during the drive home and would need lifting into the house.

That evening, while tucking them into bed, I thought back to the article about the mining boom. Although tempting, I didn't feel ready to apply for any of the jobs on offer, as I wanted to be at home each night. Although the first few weeks at the chicken factory had been unusual, I still had Sunday to recover. As for the next week–surely it couldn't be as crazy as the one before!

*

As planned, Nigel met me in the changing room at 5 a.m. on Monday morning. This time, instead of a cheeky remark or mischievous grin, all I received was a mumbled, 'Good morning.'

'What's up with you?' I asked.

'I got woken an hour ago by a call from Malcolm. He's booked a refrigerated truck to collect the chicken portions we slice, dice and box up. It arrives at ten and is driving over east, so we need to be on the ball this morning.'

I patted him on the back and said, 'Don't look so worried. At least we have some time to prepare. Come on, let's turn on the pinball machine so it can warm up before the work crew gets here.'

'Alistair, it's not a pinball machine. It's an automatic clipping machine, capable of bagging hundreds of chicken pieces per hour.'

'I hope you're right, as this is my first big test.'

The shrill of his phone caught his attention and I watched as he began pacing the room. After the call had finished, he kicked out at a nearby locker. 'That was Trevor. He works in the bagging room but won't be in today. That's the third time this month.'

'Will I get anyone else?' I asked.

'Maybe, but they'll be new and not much help. Trevor's the man we need but he's always calling in sick.'

I shrugged off the bad news and set off towards the bagging room, calling for Nigel to hurry. As I approached, he raced past me, calling out, 'Oh no! This wasn't part of the plan.'

The machine was sparkling clean, which should have cheered me up. There was just one problem. It had been dismantled over the weekend and there were parts scattered everywhere, including stainless steel legs, a shiny table, metal rods and brackets.

I pointed to the wall clock and said, 'We've got 45 minutes until that hatch opens and bits of chicken start pouring through. If you go in search of Jimmy, I'll try to figure out how it fits together.'

While I rummaged through the machine parts in search of tools and instructions, Nigel returned, along with a man I'd never seen before. 'I couldn't find Jimmy, but this is Min-soo, one of your work crew.'

Min-soo looked to be in his early forties, with a mop of dark hair and a friendly smile. After swift introductions, he observed the scene and made a dash for a cabinet to find some tools. He then called for my help to piece each section together. While adjusting the hopper, he said, 'This machine is not so good. It makes funny noises and the sides are broken.'

'You need to report each problem so we can fix them,' I said.

He smiled uneasily and lowered his voice. 'I have done that many times, but no one listens.'

'How long have you worked here?' I asked.

'I came to Australia three months ago and started here a week later.'

'What did you do in Korea for work?'

'I used to work in a chicken processing plant. Just like here, but bigger.'

'Was it as busy as here?'

'Yes, very busy, but also calm.'

'What did you do there?' I asked.

'I was an Industrial Engineer, in charge of production and quality.'

'What do you do here?' I asked.

'I mainly pack boxes and stack freezers. But today, I will try to help you out.'

While we worked together, he pointed out design flaws and worn parts in need of replacing. After we'd slotted the final piece home, he reached over and switched on the machine. At first, nothing happened until he tapped the side with a strategically placed mallet. He noticed me watching and explained. 'It has loose wiring, but Jimmy is always too busy with the other machines.'

After making a few notes, I had one final question. 'Why are you just packing boxes when you're so qualified?'

He shrugged his shoulders and said, 'I just do what I am told. When I arrived, I told them about my qualifications and tried giving advice, but they didn't listen. So now, I just watch them run around all day.'

We were interrupted by raised voices in the corridor, as the first workers arrived for their shift, stamping their feet to ward off the chill. Two young women entered the bagging room and bowed slightly as I called out a greeting. They looked towards Min-soo, who came to their aid by calling out to me. 'Alistair, they are new workers from Korea and their English is not so good. I will show them what to do and if the machine behaves, we should be okay.'

While I watched, he set them to work. One of them started preparing boxes while the other twiddled with dials on the weighing machine. The last two workers arrived with minutes to spare and instinctively hurried towards Min-soo for advice on where to start. The place had a sense of calm, and as Min-soo checked the machine, I thanked him for his help. Just as the clock struck six, the hatch at the far end of the room opened wide. Two smiling faces appeared, and one man called out, 'Which one of you is Alistair?'

I put up my hand and received the thumbs up by both men. One of them said, 'I'm Stewart and this is Damian.'

They looked to be in their early thirties, with cheerful faces and broad shoulders. Stewart then said, 'We're ready when you are. Welcome to the house of fun!'

His comment made me chuckle and it felt good to know that I wasn't the only one that thought the place was nuts. He then wheeled a metal bin to the edge of the hatch and poured the sloppy contents into the hopper. Seconds later, a raw portion of chicken appeared at the far end of the rubber conveyor. During its controlled descent, a flipper diverted the chicken fillet into one of the chutes. Many more followed in its wake–each of them flicked into designated chutes, depending on their weight or type.

The production workers then bagged the portions, before placing them into boxes, to be weighed and stamped. The first hour flew past with barely a murmur as each of us found our rhythm. Min-soo proved to be the star of the show, as he calmly assisted with each request while also trying to teach me the process.

After two hours of bliss, our luck ran out, starting with a malfunction to the weighing machine. The electronic readout faded from view and the stickers refused to spit out. While one worker interrogated the mechanism, I went in search of Jimmy. He was nowhere to be seen, and Malcolm was dealing with a fresh crisis in the freezer room.

By the time I returned, the floor underneath the machine resembled the remains of a strawberry jelly, as innards, blood and brine seeped from gaps in the metalwork. Instinctively, one worker grabbed a bucket and scrambled under the machine to catch the drips.

For all her efforts, the floor continued to turn messy, as the true scale of the damaged machine hit home. Closer investigation revealed a split in the bottom of the hopper, caused by cracked welding. While figuring out what to do next, I found a broken electrical switch, hanging by a single screw to the side of the machine. Nearby, a pool of blood flowed towards a drain.

I decided it was time to turn off the machine, but without warning the conveyor picked up speed. Suddenly the chicken parts were whizzing towards the end of the chute, leaving no time for the flippers to react. I watched in amazement as a chicken thigh flicked off the end, into mid-air.

I thrust out a hand and caught it while calling out to Min-soo to hit the emergency stop button. He was slow to react and stood to watch as two more chicken pieces catapulted off the lip of the machine. I saved the next one, but not the third, which skidded across the floor and came to a halt by the wall. Min-soo finally hit the emergency button, but the conveyor refused to stop, launching more chicken portions into orbit.

By the time we'd switched off the power supply, the floor was littered with chicken flesh. The conveyor trundled to a stop, and as the last piece of chicken dropped to the floor, the room fell silent. One worker knelt and began picking up the pieces. Without a word, we soon followed suit.

While under the conveyor, I heard a click as the door to the bagging room opened. From my low vantage point, I noticed someone entering the room. Their shiny white gumboots looked too big for Nigel and too new for Malcolm. As I contemplated my next move, a booming voice broke the silence. 'What the hell is going on?'

I crawled out from under the conveyor to find a man in his thirties holding a clipboard. His cheeks were flushed, and his eyes looked to be bulging in rage as he stabbed a finger towards me. 'Are you Alistair? What's all this? The place is a mess! What have you done?'

Without waiting for my reply, he continued to rant. 'I'm reporting this straight away. Put your hairnet back on and clean up this blood.'

It must have been displaced during my catch, but I hadn't realised. As he seethed, I couldn't help but grin. The entire scene was farcical, but I had no need to feel incompetent. I'd stayed quiet for too long, but now felt ready to share my views.

I took a breath and stepped a little nearer. 'I'd imagine your name is Bruce. Which means you must be the health and safety manager. As you can see, this machine is falling apart, just like every other one in the factory. I'm not sure what you do all day apart from walking around with a temperature gauge and a clipboard.'

He tried to speak, but I got in there first. 'These workers have been awesome today. They've worked hard without complaint, despite the crappy conditions. Did you know one of them is a qualified engineer? But we use him to pack boxes! Right now, I have an electrical fault to report, and a floor covered in blood because the machine is knackered. The order won't be ready by ten, but I get the feeling the courier is used to waiting. I suggest you either give us a hand or leave us in peace and shut the door on the way out.'

I then turned away from him and reached for a mop. As I did so, he called out, 'You're in massive trouble. Massive, I tell you.' And then he was gone.

The room fell silent for a few seconds, and then something strange happened. I got a round of applause, followed by hoots of laughter from Stewart and Damian, who'd seen and heard every word.

Stewart was leaning out of the hatch. 'Alistair, you little ripper. On the upside, you're the only person to tell him what the entire factory thinks. On the downside, he's related to the owner and I'm sorry to say this, but you're about to be history, mate.'

After cleaning up the mess, waiting for an electrician and finishing the production run, I thanked my team and went in search of something to eat. By now it was mid-afternoon and as I tucked into a sandwich, the secretary paid me a visit. She lowered her voice and said, 'Sorry, Alistair, but Nigel wants to see you.'

In the warm confines of his office, he attempted a stern face while explaining that my employment contract was no longer valid. I felt a tremendous sense of relief and held out a hand to thank him, but he couldn't meet my eyes.

As I drove out of the car park, Oliver stood by the exit alongside Nigel, his arms folded while watching my every move. My gut feeling was to spin out of the open gates in a show of boldness, but there were already enough tyre marks snaked across the tarmac. There was no need to add any more. Besides, I didn't feel any anger. Instead, I felt sorry for those left behind.

I stopped by the gates and walked over to talk with the two men. Oliver reacted uneasily, his feet shuffling as I held out a hand to thank him for the unique experience. He smiled thinly and muttered something about 'not being the right fit for the company.'

He then marched away without a backward glance, leaving me alone with Nigel. Before he had the chance to speak, I handed him the DVD of *One Flew Over the Cuckoo's Nest*. 'Nigel, I know you said it's not your type of movie, but maybe you should give it a go. I think every new employee needs to watch it as part of their induction. Once you get to the part where the Indian chief makes a dash for freedom, you'll see what I mean. By the way, if you ever find yourself pushing overloaded trolleys in the corridor, then I think it'll be too late for you.'

He looked at me blankly as I offered one last piece of advice. 'The Indian chief escaped from the madhouse and ran for his life. It's not too late for you to do something similar.'

He kept his eyes on the DVD as I returned to my car and drove away, feeling a sense of relief as the factory dwindled from view in my rear mirror. I'd moved to Australia for the chance of an adventure, but catching chicken thighs in mid-air wasn't the type of escapade I'd been searching for.

Maybe the iron ore mines in the Pilbara region would suit me better. With this thought in mind, I headed home to tell Fran that I was out of a job again. Six months after my departure, they put the factory into receivership, and it now stands empty. It was three months before I could eat chicken again.

EXIT
JW

Beautiful World

"The greatest threat to our planet is the belief that someone else will save it."

– Robert Swan

The chilly escapades in the chicken factory led to a snap decision to skip ten days of a breezy southwest winter, for a place in the sun with my family. Our destination was the coastal town of Exmouth, famed as the gateway to the UNESCO, World Heritage Listed, Ningaloo Reef. It is the world's longest fringing reef, stretching 260 kilometres along the northwest coast, and the surrounding waters are renowned for the annual spectacle when hundreds of whale sharks pass through during their migration, to coincide with a mass spawning of coral.

The 1,400-kilometre road trip would take us north, beyond a circular line of latitude, known as the Tropic of Capricorn. This is one of five major parallels of latitude you'll find on a map or globe and marks the southernmost point on Earth where the sun is directly overhead at noon, during the December solstice. It is located approximately 23 degrees south of the equator and we planned to cross the invisible marker during day two of our journey. Once crossed, we'd leave behind the Southern Temperate Zone, in favour of the tropics, where warm and sunny days are the norm between May and September.

The idea of visiting Ningaloo had come from a Melbourne taxi driver I'd met on our arrival into Australia many years earlier. A lot had happened since then, including the birth of our two children, and the time now seemed perfect to take a trip to the reef. Tagging along would be Fran's brother, Russell, and his family. He'd recently moved to Perth with his wife, Michelle, and their young children, Oliver and Eve. This was to be our first Australian road trip together!

Travelling 2,800-kilometres for a ten-day round-trip is something Australians seem to take in their stride, but a search on Google Maps reminded me that a similar escapade across Britain could encompass a return trip from Brighton, on the south coast of England, to the northern tip of mainland Scotland, where the remote village of John O'Groats overlooks the wild Atlantic. Such a trip could be deemed ambitious, expensive and arduous, especially during the UK school holidays, when millions of people hit the roads. Unpredictable weather, varying terrain and painstaking roadworks add to the mix, along with the multitude of towns, villages, and cities to either bypass or navigate.

According to my road map, there was only one highway heading north along the West Australian coast and far fewer towns to deal with compared to those between Brighton and John O'Groats. Instead of traffic jams, road rage and inclement weather, our challenges would be very different.

Although we were travelling along sealed roads, the vast distances between road houses–for fuel, coffee and snacks–and coastal communities–to stretch our legs and rest for the night–warranted the need to load up on drinking water–especially if we broke down between any of the pit stops. We also needed to consider the perils of hitting kangaroos, especially if driving between dusk and dawn.

Before we left, I packed a box set of road trip CDs to keep us entertained between sightings of emus, camels, kangaroos and broken-down campervans! Best of all–each vehicle had a two-way radio, so we could stay in touch while driving in convoy.

During two days of driving, the clouds dispersed, and the weather warmed as we inched our way north. As expected, the road trip included stops for coffee, snacks and fuel, along with changes of driver, leg stretches, back stretches, toilet dashes and an overnight stay in a budget motel, followed many hours later by a photo alongside a roadside sign, declaring we'd made it to the Tropic of Capricorn.

Not long after, we stopped to admire a giant prawn, four metres tall, looming by the side of the road. Made from fibreglass and steel, the pink crustacean stood proud against the clear blue sky, in recognition of the world-renowned sustainable fishery which annually harvests 900 tonnes of wild prawns from local waters. With thoughts about fishing trips, prawns on the barbeque and sunset drinks by the ocean, we left behind the colourful sculpture and went in search of our campsite.

Our first day in Exmouth was a chilled one, relishing family time in the camp pool while soaking up the sun, along with many others that had made the long drive north. Apart from families enjoying a school holiday break, there was another type of traveller in the camp. These looked older, ranging in age from their fifties to their eighties, with weathered faces touched by the sun, as they strolled casually between ablution blocks and the kitchen, dressed in faded shorts and T-shirts.

These, I discovered were *Grey Nomads*, renowned as adventurous retirees following the sun year-round. Throughout the first afternoon, I caught sight of many other *Grey Nomads* scattered around camp, either lounging outside their caravans, reading, sipping drinks, or chatting with other travellers. Some spent time repairing or adjusting parts of their caravan rigs. Others dozed, hung washing on lines, or sat in the shade of their awnings, watching TV on screens far bigger than the one I had at home.

That evening, while at the communal kitchen on plate cleaning duties, I chatted to a sprightly couple called Tom and Hazel, who were circumnavigating the country in celebration of their recent retirements. Hazel had spent many years as a high school teacher and Tom had recently hung his tools up, after thirty years as a diesel mechanic. Their children had flown the nest and they were now on the road, in search of adventure with the help of an off-road caravan, filled with features including solar panels, a shower and air conditioning.

While I scrubbed plates, they sat nearby, sipping wine and sharing travel stories, including a secret spot they were keen to reveal if only there was a map at hand! I also learned about the camaraderie on the open road between *Grey Nomads,* helping with directions, offering advice, and making plans for sunset drinks.

As I dried the dishes, they shared a tale about a recent sunset, with clouds ablaze and far-reaching views of untouched beaches, while they camped in nearby dunes. They'd since travelled into town for a few creature comforts and the chance to catch up on emails, wash clothes and restock their pantry. Soon, they'd be on the road again, keen to escape the crowded camp and boisterous children!

While packing away the dishes, I asked for advice on where to go on a family day trip. Turquoise Bay won their vote, as they described the sparkling waters teeming with fish, lapping against a crescent beach of velvety sand, perfect for kids and as warm as toast. Just as I left the kitchen, Tom called out, 'Don't forget to take a snorkel and mask and watch out for the sharks!'

Later that evening, with the children tucked up in bed, I sat outside the tent with Fran. The night air was warm, with barely a murmur across the camp, except a gentle breeze stirring the leaves of a nearby tree. Fran had set the scene, with drinks on hand, along with cheese, crackers and soft music.

As I lounged in my camp chair, a cold beer in one hand, a headtorch at the ready, I reached for the tourist pamphlets collected earlier from camp reception. A complimentary map displayed the surrounding coastline, including locations to fish, snorkel, or scuba dive. Within the giveaways, I discovered a range of activities on offer, including skydiving and deep-sea fishing. There was also the chance to swim alongside whale sharks, the largest species of fish in the world.

These elusive creatures usually grow to 12 metres, although some mature males have been measured at 20 metres, with an estimated weight of 20 tonnes! Such an excursion would involve charter boats, spotter planes and the signing of disclaimer forms and although appealing, was beyond my budget. Instead, I planned a simpler and cheaper adventure, in Turquoise Bay, for the chance to snorkel on Ningaloo Reef, with over 500 species of fish inhabiting the protected waters.

I also found a passage in my guidebook about reef sharks, which sparked Fran's interest as she poured more wine and sat back to listen. 'It says here that Turquoise Bay is home to black-tip reef sharks which are–get this–*unintentionally dangerous, with a timid and skittish nature*.'

The topic of sharks prompted her to remind me of my swimming abilities. 'Ali, please stay close to shore, away from any type of shark, even timid ones!'

Twelve hours later, both families were in convoy again, this time for a shorter road trip, into Cape Range National Park, which adjoins the pristine and protected waters of Ningaloo Marine Park. I'd expected to find a crowded beach, filled with families enjoying the sunshine, but our early arrival at Turquoise Bay proved to be a relaxed one as we staked our claim on a stretch of pure white sand. As Fran and Michelle laid out a blanket, Russell reached for a book in preparation of a leisurely read. The children were itching to get into the water and with promises to take them soon I made my excuses and dashed towards the shoreline.

By the time I'd slipped on my fins, I was joined by Fran and the children, who watched as I walked backwards into the clear water while holding a snorkel and mask. With each step, schools of tiny fish darted past my ankles. As I adjusted my mask, Fran called out, 'Have fun, but don't go too far!'

I gave them a wave before turning my attention to a colourful school of fish taking a wide berth around my legs. Instead of being in the Indian Ocean, I could have been in an aquarium, and was only a few metres from shore. Before setting off, I spotted two swimmers in the distance, each using a snorkel and mask. They were venturing further out to sea and with plans to follow suit I took a breath and kicked off from the sand in search of Ningaloo Reef!

As sunlight danced on the warm, turquoise water, I floated face down to observe the sea life below. Just a few metres away lay a colourful world, alive with seagrass and schools of resident fish. For a while I drifted leisurely, taking my time to enjoy the underwater scene while passing over untouched coral. At times, I came across other snorkellers, and we'd float side by side, enjoying the sun on our backs while searching for movement below.

With so much to see, we'd then drift apart, each person drawn to something different on the reef. While studying the seabed, I spotted an octopus in transit across the ocean floor. I sucked in a lungful of air, dived towards the sea creature and watched it change colour as it came to a patch of sand.

After returning to the surface for air, I swam back towards the octopus, but came face to face with a loggerhead turtle instead, its wizened eyes staring into mine. With apparent ease, it changed direction and glided over a coral outcrop. I tried keeping up, but it dived deeper, leaving me alone and breathless.

That was when I noticed the fearsome outline of a shark carving through the water. Even from afar, I could see its steely eyes, iron-grey skin and black-tipped fin. With my chest tightening, I raced to the surface and caught my breath. Although I knew from my guidebook it was a placid creature, my mind raced with terrifying thoughts in case it changed direction and headed my way.

Crazily, I was still close to shore and could hear children's laughter wafting on the summer breeze, which prompted me to search for Fran among the handful of holidaymakers enjoying the sunshine. She was sitting near the water's edge, scooping sand into a bucket, cajoling our two young boys into play. I flapped my arms and with a sixth sense she looked up and called out, 'Hey boys, there's Dad, give him a wave.'

There was no time to reply as I turned my attention to the shark, which had moved in a wide circle around me! Earlier, there'd been other swimmers nearby, but they'd seemingly vanished during the last few minutes. So too, had the shark. Eyes wide, I glanced left, right and below, thinking back to the words in my guidebook, describing black-tip reef sharks as, *unintentionally dangerous, with a timid and skittish nature.*

While peering across the reef, I found it again, slowly circling, keeping its distance without a hint of being timid or skittish. Maybe it was just curious of the solo swimmer within easy reach of its razor-sharp teeth! Fighting the urge to panic, I turned towards the beach and made a bid for safety. With each determined stroke, the surrounding water became shallower until I reached a sandbar, which allowed me to stand with ease. Although close to the beach, there was still one more hurdle to tackle, a four-metre-wide channel that ran parallel with the shoreline. After taking a breath, I leapt into the water, feeling the force of the current while floating close to land.

That was when I saw the shark again, its dark fin carving through the water as it sped through the channel. There was no time to react, and as my body tensed, the edge of its tail brushed across my stomach. After it slipped below the waterline, I scrambled onto the beach, gasping for breath as

Fran appeared by my side, asking where I'd been for the last hour! In response, I ran a finger across my stomach, tracing the narrow graze left by the shark's tail. She reached out to touch it and said, 'What happened? Did you brush against the coral?'

'No, I just had a close encounter with a shark!'

'Oh, you are funny. Come on, we've been waiting for you and are about to eat.'

After a mid-morning snack, I was enticed back into the water by Fran and the children, to play in the shallows. Once again, the sea life came close, causing giggles from the boys as schools of silvery fish darted between our legs.

Over the next five days, we juggled our time between the camp pool and the surrounding beaches. During one special moment, we discovered a lonely beach and watched as loggerhead turtles swam past, their heads popping out of the water for a breath of air as we stood in awe and tried counting them all.

To break up the homeward journey, we headed south towards the coastal settlement of Monkey Mia, famed for its daily visits of wild bottlenose dolphins for over 50 years. During the drive, Fran reminisced about her previous escapades in Australia, while in her twenties. Together with a mixed bag of other backpackers, she'd travelled overland from the east coast towards Perth. The man at the wheel had been Don, who completed the trip each year so that he could visit his daughter.

Those on board helped pay for the fuel, while Don acted as a tour guide and cook, taking them to little-known places off the beaten track. After many weeks of travel, including time in Perth, they'd casually headed north along the coast of Western Australia. A few days after pitching her tent close to the beach at Monkey Mia, Fran fell under its magical spell, with its golden sands, turquoise water, endless skies and star-filled nights. Most of all, she became captivated by the dolphins.

Despite the basic setup, she stayed for many days, lapping up the sunshine while chatting with travellers from across the world. The beachside campsite had few amenities, except an outside shower, toilet block, communal kitchen and barbeque. When Don announced he was on the move again, Fran decided to stay put.

Along with a handful of campers, she stood in the shallows each morning, waiting for dolphins to arrive. Sometimes there would be a pod of five or six within touching distance. On other mornings or late in the afternoon, just a few would appear from the deep. Occasionally, none would show.

No one knows for sure how Monkey Mia got its unusual name, but there are many theories. Some believe that '*Monkey*' comes from the name of a pearling boat that moored close by during the mid-nineteenth century. '*Mia*' is an Aboriginal term for shelter. Maybe the pearling boat anchored offshore, waiting for a storm to pass, before resuming its voyage.

We travelled in less adventurous fashion, on a desert road, with both cars in convoy and the two-way radio in constant use, to keep the passengers entertained. After turning off the highway, we approached the coastal town of Denham by navigating a palm-fringed roundabout. The ocean was rarely far from sight, stretching into the distance, with boats of every size in motion, including luxury yachts and a fishing trawler. Soon after, we passed a caravan park with million-dollar views and stopped by a supermarket to grab provisions.

The air felt warm and breezy, tasting of salt and sea spray, tempting me to remain outside. While the families navigated air-conditioned aisles in search of healthy greens and sunset snacks, I stood by the water's edge, watching a fisherman chug past in an aluminium boat.

We'd entered Shark Bay World Heritage Area, incorporating over two million hectares of coast and ocean. Within these waters, you'll discover one of the largest seagrass meadows in the world, proving a perfect habitat for dugongs, sharks, turtles and rays. Dugongs are placid creatures, similar in length to dolphins, but slightly wider and without a fin. They have shovelled snouts and eat up to 50 kilograms of seagrass a day, which is a reason they are often known as sea cows!

The children emerged from the shop with ice creams, which kept them occupied as we loaded up with essentials. We then made our way along a sealed road towards Monkey Mia. There were no hills or ridges to navigate, just a flat, sunburned landscape, dotted with hardy spinifex. During the late afternoon drive, we spotted a fully grown kangaroo far ahead, bouncing across the empty road, with no thought of looking left or right. Within three hops, it had vanished into the surrounding bush, followed by a sprightly joey, taking far more hops to cover the same distance. The youngster didn't look around either, oblivious to the near miss with our car bonnet!

As the sun dropped lower, I kept my speed to a minimum, searching the surrounding scrub for signs of wildlife. In the fading light, Fran caught sight of a road sign for Monkey Mia and in that moment the memories flooded back. As we drew nearer to the campsite, she said, 'I can't believe I'm here again, after so many years. I loved the beauty, the dolphins and the isolation. The night sky was amazing, with millions of stars and absolute silence, apart from tiny waves lapping the sand.'

She then blinked away the memory, her voice turning serious. 'They say you shouldn't go back to places you once loved. I hope it hasn't changed too much over the years.'

A day later, she gave me her verdict. 'It's busier than I remember, and I never expected to see a bar and restaurant all the way out here. There used to be a statue of a dolphin on the grass, which seems to be gone. But the swimming pool looks great and the beachfront is still breath-taking.'

The camping spot she'd once had to herself was now home to a two-bedroom chalet, complete with hot running water and ocean views from a shady veranda. There were many other units in the same complex and we snapped up the last two mid-range family cabins, which meant hot showers and the chance to watch TV, but no ocean views.

The beach was only a two-minute walk from our door and on the first morning, with Fran and the boys sleeping, I crept outside with tea and toast. I stepped onto the beach just after dawn, greeted by the faint swirl of pink clouds far above, with hardly a breath of wind to stir the ocean. Despite my early alarm, I wasn't the first to arrive. To my left was a young man with a camera and tripod, focused on capturing the moment.

Minutes later, a barefooted fisherman appeared on the beach, wearing a singlet and shorts. He ambled past while holding a bucket and rod, greeting me with a friendly nod, followed by, 'G'day, mate.'

He kept on walking along the rust-red sand, his footprints the first of the day to make an imprint. I stayed put, my eyes on the sparkling water, hoping to spot dolphins. The only sign of wildlife was a solitary pelican, paddling after the fisherman. While finishing my tea, I strolled onto a nearby jetty to admire the smooth lines of a moored catamaran, offering wildlife cruises later that day. I then sat with my legs dangling over the wharf, enjoying the rising sun on my face.

I must have closed my eyes and didn't notice the mum and toddler approaching from the holiday park. They broke the silence as the child called out, 'Mummy, look, a dolphin.'

In an instant, I sat upright, opened my eyes and shielded them from the sun. The first thing I noticed was a youngster, dressed in a matching vest and shorts, pointing towards a nearby dolphin. It was moving slowly in the water, its mouth open, as if to greet the smiling boy.

The boy's mother was trying to capture the moment with a camera, while I remained seated, smiling at our good fortune. For a few valuable minutes, it was just the four of us. I stayed perfectly still, resisting the urge to rush from the jetty to stand closer. Soon after, another dolphin appeared, slightly smaller, cruising the shallows from a safe distance. This time, I made a dash to our cabin, to find Fran with the boys, munching on toast and asking why I was out of breath.

Ten minutes later, with Seby in my arms and Noah racing ahead with Fran, we made our way to the beach. During that time, a handful of other guests had followed suit, each of them standing barefoot in the shallows, looking for signs of life in the water. I spotted the mum from earlier, now carrying her child and smiling as she walked towards me. 'Weren't we lucky to be there! They've just gone, but hopefully they'll come back soon.'

The boys didn't seem bothered by the lack of dolphins and after a quick splash, happily headed home to finish their breakfast. We returned to the beach an hour later, as advised by a pamphlet in our room, and discovered a different scene altogether! A long line of barefoot visitors was being called to order by a blonde-haired woman wearing a bright T-shirt, depicting her role as a volunteer. Close by, a man was plugging cables into a portable amplifier, before checking for sound on his microphone. 'Testing, one, two.'

Most onlookers were standing ankle-deep in the shallows, forming a ragged line that stretched for 30 metres. Fran and the boys joined the queue, while I walked behind the line of people, searching between gaps for any signs of dolphins. A man in a baseball cap controlled the front of the line. He also wore a bright T-shirt, and I watched as he reached down to feed a waiting dolphin. Fran and the boys, 30 metres to my left, were oblivious to the moment, but could soon hear the running commentary from the loudspeaker. 'Good morning, everyone. Welcome to Monkey Mia. For over 50 years...'

All at once, the ambience changed. Instead of listening to waves lap on the beach, all I could hear was an amplified voice crackling through a speaker. In that moment, I thought back to a time long ago, while at Machu Picchu, after trekking along the Inca Trail with Fran. After four days tackling mountain passes and remote valleys, we'd arrived during the stillness of dawn and for a few precious hours explored the famous ruins, along with many other trekkers.

By midday, the ancient city had become overrun with thousands of visitors that had arrived by train and bus, all hustling for space. Local guides chaperoned them into herds, some using portable loudspeakers to gain their attention. The peace and tranquillity of the mountains had been lost, as tourists and tour guides shouted to be heard amongst the throng and excitement.

Although not as extreme, the beachside scene at Monkey Mia reminded me of that long ago moment. But from what I could see, most of those lining up to view the dolphins didn't seem disturbed by the running commentary. To escape the noise, I kept walking along the beach, my eyes on the lone fisherman a few hundred metres away. As I approached, he cast his line into the water and turned to face me. 'Had enough of the loudspeaker, mate?'

'How did you guess?'

'Just figured. I saw you this morning, and you probably got to see dolphins without the need to line up. As for the loudspeaker and feeding of dolphins, I just don't get it. I think they call it ecotourism or some other name. I've been coming here since I was a kid, but it's different now. I used to camp by the beach, and at night we'd build fires from driftwood and there was always someone with a guitar. It's still a top spot and is great for children, with a pool and playground. But I enjoy being somewhere wilder and quieter.'

That afternoon, the boys played with their cousins while the adults prepared drinks and nibbles. Just before sunset we headed to the beach, in search of a place to spread our picnic rug. This time there was no line-up of people, or a man with a microphone and loudspeaker. There was talk from a nearby couple that dolphins were due in soon, but our sights were set on a row of anglers further ahead.

The fisherman I'd spoken to at sunrise was amongst them. He still wore the same singlet and shorts, but now sported a baseball cap and sunglasses, while holding a beer in one hand and a rod in the other. A young girl of about ten cast her line as I walked alongside, but while pulling in the slack, it caught on a nearby buoy. As she struggled to free it, I heard her dad call out. 'Wait a second, and I'll help.'

In the last of the light, with barely a ripple on the water, it seemed a perfect time for a swim. I grabbed the attention of her dad while pulling off my T-shirt. 'I'm happy to help and the dip will cool me down.'

The man passed his rod to a friend and walked towards me, smiling while shaking his head. 'That's not a good idea, mate. Do you know why this place is called Shark Bay?'

The answer had to be obvious, but it was only as I spoke the words out loud that reality hit home. 'Well, I suppose it has something to do with sharks.'

He smiled again. 'You're learning fast, mate. There are loads of sharks and some get close to shore. Don't worry about the fishing hook. I'll sort it, no problem.'

Fran came to my rescue, calling out from our picnic rug, which was now laden with a selection of cheeses, crackers and dips. After making my excuses to the fisherman, I settled on the rug, beer in hand, while enjoying the ocean scene. Partway through my drink, the fisherman called out to me. 'Here mate, take a look at this.'

I stepped closer and followed his gaze towards the clear water. Just a few metres away, a patrolling shark passed by. My eyes were drawn to its broad head and wide mouth, which opened slightly to reveal a flash of razor-sharp teeth. It had a long, slender body, with grey stripes and a powerful tail which moved slowly through the water. It looked to be scouting the seabed and stayed within view for a few minutes, until, with a flick of its tail, set off for deeper waters. As I stood silently by the shore, the man patted me on the back and lowered his voice. 'Bet you don't get four-metre tiger sharks in Margate, mate. That thing could chomp you in two within seconds.'

As the shark continued its journey, I returned to our picnic, watching the blood-red sun dip towards the horizon. I'd only been in Monkey Mia a day and was already hooked!

Far from Home

"The pay is good and I can walk to work."
– John F. Kennedy

While living in England I used many forms of transportation during my trips to work, including bike, train and car. I even tried cross-country skiing to the Vauxhall factory one morning, when a wintry whiteout closed all the local roads. One mode of transport I rarely used was an airplane, as most companies that I worked for were relatively close by.

In a country as vast as Australia you get used to travelling long distances, especially if your work takes you out of town. It is estimated that eight percent of the Australian population fly to work, and after my escapades at the chicken factory, I applied for a job in the mines.

China's insatiable demand for resources has created opportunities in the northwest of Australia, as large tracts of land are mined for their iron ore, transported overland to Port Hedland and then shipped to East Asia. The mining companies require thousands of workers on these sites, to extract, process and ship the ore. Most fly from Perth to a region known as the Pilbara, where they live in purpose-built camps and work twelve-hour shifts for weeks at a time. Australians have termed this style of working as FIFO, meaning Fly-In-Fly-Out.

My job application led to a brief phone call with a busy career consultant, followed by an hour long, two-panel interview in a city centre meeting room. Days later, I was asked to complete a psychometric test, along with a detailed medical. After finding out that I'd passed them both, there was one last hurdle to overcome. My potential boss was keen for me to spend a day and night in one of the remote sites before committing further, to see what I thought of the experience. He also wanted my potential teammates to meet me, to see if they thought I'd fit in with the culture and work-life balance.

This is how I came to be at Perth airport at 5 a.m. one February morning, queuing for coffee alongside a row of miners. Most were dressed for work, in fluorescent shirts, jeans and steel-capped boots. The customer in front of me was a wide-shouldered Māori, who gave enthusiastic high fives to passing colleagues as they headed towards the buffet area. On his back was a small rucksack, inscribed with the words, *Safety Comes First*. Although the lounge was also filled with those on business and a handful of holidaymakers, it was the colourful miners who stole my attention.

We boarded on time but took off late. The pilot apologised for the delay, but none of the passengers looked upset. Within minutes of being airborne, I gazed below at the city centre, where skyscrapers twinkled in the first rays of sunlight, the tallest belonging to resource companies and the banking sector.

The city is split in two by the Swan River and as I studied the wide expanse of water, boats of every type could be seen, including a ferry in transit from South Perth to the city centre. At this hour, the city was stirring to life, with cars and trucks jostling for position on a three-lane highway. If any drivers were to look up, they'd see a plane heading into the desert, away from suburbia, filled with FIFO commuters.

From my window seat I glimpsed the waterside cranes in Fremantle harbour, followed by a sighting of Rottnest Island, the low-lying island sitting below a blanket of mist. We were now above the Indian Ocean, with a clear view of a line of cargo ships, each one waiting for a call from the Port of Fremantle.

The pilot dipped the wings and we veered north, towards Hillary's Boat Harbour and its luxury yachts, lined up in neat rows. Minutes later, we flew over the newly built suburbs, their metal rooftops shining in the early light. The houses stretched into the distance, clinging to the lucrative shoreline.

The new estates finally gave way to greenery, until the pilot banked again, this time into the arid interior. We flew above dried riverbeds, carved by seasonal rains over millennia. We were still relatively low, which gave me time to search for off-road tracks, created by those looking to escape the city. As we increased in altitude, the tracks dwindled from view. Soon, the terrain looked unforgiving and uninhabited.

The flight took two hours and most on board rarely stirred from their seats. Some passengers sat quietly, their eyes closed, while others watched movies on laptops or other devices. As the plane descended, I cast my eyes to the scene below. We were above the Pilbara, a vast semi-desert still inhabited by settlements of Aboriginals, the traditional owners of the land. Some work in the mines and Aboriginal elders frequently negotiate with those who wish to extract the natural resources.

While approaching the airport, we flew above a series of rolling hills, each one parched from the sun. The land between each ridge looked to be claret red, with pockets of greenery alongside the jagged scar of a dried riverbed. As the plane banked for the last time, I spotted the active mining area, where yellow trucks trundled along dusty roads with their valuable cargo. From a thousand feet up, they resembled Tonka toys, but up close and personal they are taller than a double-decker bus. With high iron ore prices, the Pilbara is a rewarding place to do business, if you can manage the risks and operating costs.

The airport was a simple affair. There was one landing strip, overlooked by a row of metal-clad buildings, modified for use as waiting rooms and a check-in terminal. After a perfect landing, the passengers stirred to life, and as soon as we'd come to a halt they were on their feet. For most on board, this was just the start of another long stint on the mines, but to me it offered the possibility of a new career.

After stepping outside, a blast of warm air greeted me, followed by a buzzing of flies as I made my way down the steps in blinding light. I was still trying to wave insects away when I noticed a man standing by the perimeter gate, holding up a placard with my name on it. As I approached, he held out a hand to greet me. 'Hi, Alistair. I'm Tim. Welcome to the Pilbara. How was the flight? I hear this is your first time on the mines, so we'll go for a tour and have a chat along the way. It's going to be a warm one today, nudging into the thirties by lunchtime. How do you cope in the heat?'

I didn't want to mention that my throat already felt parched, although I'd only been off the plane for two minutes. I tried ignoring the flies by my face and gave a confident smile. 'Well, Tim, as you can probably tell by my accent, I'm a long way from England. We had a heatwave there in the summer of 76, which I survived as a kid.'

'That's good to hear, Alistair. I'm also a blow-in, after moving from Zimbabwe years ago. We seem to attract many characters up here, from all over the world.'

While we'd been talking, the other passengers had collected their bags and were now on board the waiting buses. There was just one holdall left on the trailer. Tim picked it up and led me to a mud-stained four-wheel drive, parked in a designated bay.

I got to sit shotgun as he waited for the last bus to pull away, before edging behind at a safe distance, chatting away to me as if we were old friends. By the time we'd arrived at the main camp, I'd learned about the small gold mine he'd once owned and operated, until seized by the Zimbabwean government. Despite the apparent loss of a fortune, he was rarely without a smile, with craggy features and a shock of blonde hair, greying at the temples.

While at camp, he waited patiently as I drank from a water cooler, then led me to the shade of nearby trees to point out buildings of interest and key features. Pride of place belonged to a row of barbeques, surrounded by wooden benches. These, I learned, were in demand most evenings, overlooking a stretch of lush grass, watered at intervals throughout day and night and kept trim by maintenance staff.

As I gazed around, he led me to a safety fence and said, 'The pool is over there, along with the gym. Don't worry if you spot the resident goanna patrolling the grounds as he mainly hunts snakes and will leave you alone. Mind you, he's about a metre long with impressive claws and a deadly bite!'

While my mind raced at the thought of coming face to face with such a creature, Tim gave me a tour of the air-conditioned gym. It was kitted out with all the essentials and in use by a night shift worker, pounding a treadmill before heading to bed.

On the way to the canteen, we passed a group of men sitting around a table, littered with opened beer cans. I caught one man stifling a yawn as he cracked open another can, before taking a long swig. Tim noticed me staring and said, 'They've just finished their night shift and are allowed a few drinks, even though it's early in the morning. Personally, I think they're mad, but if it helps them unwind, then good luck to them.'

We left the off-duty miners to their beers and made our way to the canteen, which was filled to near capacity with hundreds of weary and hungry night shift workers. Some tucked into platefuls of eggs, bacon, beans and toast, chatting away to those around them. Others sat alone, their eyes on the overhead TV screen. I glanced up and caught sight of the weekly weather forecast, with sunshine all the way and a high of 40 degrees by midweek.

While I waited for the busy chef to conjure up a Spanish omelette, Tim picked a handful of grapes and offered some advice. 'If you get a job offer, then stick to a healthy diet and don't get lured by the cakes and pies. It's easy to put on weight up here, as the food is varied and plentiful. I have a blowout once a week, normally on a Sunday, when I have a few beers and play pool with friends. I visit the gym most evenings or go for a walk around the nature track to mix it up a little.'

After a safety brief, Tim kitted me out with a high-viz vest, hard hat and work boots, before making a move towards the office block to meet some of the engineers, support staff and technicians. As we wound our way along a warren of corridors, he seemed to know most workers by name. He stopped a few times, either to introduce me to a friend or colleague or to highlight where the differing teams met each morning before commencing their shift.

The walls for each meeting room were filled with charts and task boards, with lots of red and green dots depicting the highs, lows and current issues requiring attention. In other places, I spotted safety posters, their topics wide ranging, including the need to check the colour of your urine every time you pee!

Our next location required a short drive along a dirt road and after parking up, he handed over ear protectors and safety glasses, with a warning to keep them on at all times. We were soon climbing a set of metal steps, surrounded by a mass of steel columns, crushers and conveyors. After we'd arrived at the top, Tim pointed out potential hazards such as hosepipes and scaffold poles, tucked to one side in readiness for a planned task. While he spoke, the platform vibrated, along with every other piece of metalwork within view. All around was dust and noise, as the ore was pounded into submission by giant crushers or shaken to bits before being transported by conveyor to the next stage of the process.

As I took in the scene, Tim raised his voice and gave me a rundown. 'We're on top of the ore processing facility, otherwise known as the OPF. It cost millions to construct and has a capacity of forty million tonnes per year.'

He then explained about the need to run the OPF all day and night, to ensure the iron ore was stockpiled in time for the freight trains. While I digested the logistics of such an endeavour, he led me to the far side of the platform, away from the clatter of machinery. 'I love the view from up here. My favourite time is sunset when the rocks come to life.'

In response, I waved flies from my sweaty face, gave an enthusiastic nod and peered across the Martian landscape.

The 30-metre vantage point gave us the chance to spot giant haul trucks in the distance, each one kicking up red dirt as they made their way towards a designated dumping ground.

Tim pointed towards the nearest truck and raised his voice again. 'They have a payload of 250 tonnes and the trains we own are some of the longest and heaviest in the world, capable of moving 30,000 tonnes of ore in one go. They take about five hours to reach Port Hedland. From there, cargo ships transport hundreds of thousands of tonnes to China each week, for the steel mills.'

He then led me away from the rumble of a wide conveyor, filled with football-sized lumps of reddish ore. 'So, Alistair, what do you think of it so far?'

I didn't dare tell him my real thoughts. This was way out of my comfort zone and a far cry from my normal mode of work. Each piece of machinery seemed to be worth millions of dollars and the constant wear and harsh climate would pay havoc on productivity. The flies and heat were relentless, with a glaring sun that seemed to grow stronger as the day wore on.

Despite these grievances, there was also something magical about the place! There was a sense of purpose, a drive to get things done in extreme conditions and a warmth from each worker I met during the tour, including the mine manager, shift supervisors and the team I was looking to join.

The tour from Tim had opened my eyes to the frustrations and challenges faced by those working so far from home and I was keen to help. The adjustment to life as a FIFO miner would take time, but I was ready to pounce if they offered the job. With this in mind, I gave him the best response I could muster, including a rundown of my skills and experience while working in a car plant, looking to improve productivity and maintenance.

Thankfully, he nodded in response as we made our way down the steps towards his vehicle. Along the way, we passed two maintenance workers, lugging parts to a broken conveyor. As we watched them go, Tim turned to me and said, 'They built this place in a hurry to take advantage of high iron ore prices, but we're too wasteful and need to improve. Where was the last place you worked?'

I smiled at the memory and said, 'A chicken factory, close to home. Things didn't work out as I'd planned, hence my application to work on the mines.'

'Sounds like a *fowl* job,' he joked, before getting serious once again and asking if I had any more questions.

By sunset, I was back at camp, fighting the urge to smile after getting the nod of approval from Tim and my new boss. Compared to the chaotic days at the chicken factory, this was a game changer, offering the chance of a decent wage and a meaningful career path. As my mind whirred with possibilities, Tim headed to the gym, towel and water bottle in hand, calling out that he'd drive me to the airport in the morning. After a celebratory meal of steak and chips, I found a quiet corner of the bar to enjoy a cold beer.

The outdoor area was filled with benches and tables, where off-duty miners sat side by side, drinking beers while sharing stories about their day. Although the sun had gone down, the heat refused to budge, despite the efforts of a metre-wide fan whirring at full speed. There was even a jukebox, belting out a selection of rock and pop classics. The inside bar was cooler and quieter, with pool and darts on offer, plus a kiosk selling papers, magazines and snacks.

Despite the music and laughter, the tavern closed at 8.30, just as it did every evening. Rules are strict and every employee would be breath-tested for alcohol before they started work in the morning. Those that fail are escorted from the mine site, never to return.

I returned to the mine a month later, this time as a full-time employee. I soon discovered that I'd secured an enviable role, to assist the business with improving its operations. As an introduction, I was given a free rein during the first week, which meant getting out and about to explore the mine and meet the people that made it tick. During my first weekend, I spent time in the surrounding bushland with one of the environmental team, checking traps for feral cats and wild dogs.

During our time away, Andy shared his passion for wildlife and the challenges of working remotely. I also gained an insight into the duties of an environmental officer, which included education to all workers about recycling, water use and the risk of ground contamination from fuel spills.

Late in the afternoon, he drove me to a vantage point to enjoy tea from a flask. It felt good to be away from the hustle of the camp and in the silence we used high-powered binoculars to scan distant treetops, hoping to spot an endangered species of parrot. Instead of bird sightings, we discovered the fresh tracks of a snake, close to where we sat.

To kick start my first project, I sat high above the ground in air-conditioned comfort, alongside operators in charge of million-dollar dump trucks and diggers. I'd been tasked with measuring cycle times and streamlining the end-to-end process of drilling, blasting, digging and transporting the ore. Not only did I collect valuable data, but also heard the latest gossip about life on the camp.

The first operator I met had once been a primary school teacher until worn down by unruly children and the constant marking of after-hours homework. Now she worked half the year, for twice her previous salary. Another truck driver mentioned he was studying for a degree, with informative podcasts playing from a speaker as he drove in circles each day, collecting and unloading ore.

I also met a fixed-plant electrician who'd been working at the mine for five years. With a chuckle, he shared a few tales about the early days, before the construction of the pool, gym and café. 'The place was pretty basic back then, but you could still get a few beers and a decent feed after work. One thing's for sure, there were far fewer rules. Nowadays, we have heaps of paperwork to complete before each job, which is meant to make us safer.'

Through each workplace encounter, I learned a little more about the culture of the mine, but soon discovered that life there was not all about high wages, ample food, and the chance to enjoy the after-work amenities. Early alarms were required, sometimes from 4 a.m. to meet with the specialised crew who carried out drilling and blasting. The workers toiled each day under a relentless sun, marking the pit floor, digging bore holes into the caked earth and taking ore samples for lab technicians.

Each worker wore high-viz neck protectors connected to the back of their hard hats and most carried backpacks filled with water, to ensure they could stay hydrated while on the job. After spending three days with them, I got pulled to one side by the supervisor. 'They're a good bunch, who work hard and I'm sure you've noticed the frustrations we get while out here each day. As this is your last shift with this crew, I've got a surprise. If you want to see a blast in action, go and find Curly. He's the blast controller and will take you for a ride this afternoon.'

Curly, as I'd guessed, was a bald man, with broad shoulders and a bone-crushing handshake. He led me to his four-wheel drive and asked me to buckle up. Seemingly happy, he then made a series of quick-fire calls to work colleagues about the upcoming blast, then switched channels on the two-way radio. Finally, he switched on a siren and flashing beacon before turning his attention towards me. 'Mate, do you know the speed limit in the active mine?'

'I think it's thirty kilometres an hour.'

'Spot on, mate. But not for you and me! We're about to blast an area the size of two footy fields and this is the last check to ensure the place is cleared.'

With that, he sped off, grinning widely as we raced past a speed sign. Hours earlier the mining area had been a hive of activity, but as we traversed the wide stretch of open cut ground and surrounding dirt roads, there was no sign of machinery or people. Fifteen minutes later we were safely behind a set of red cones, with a perfect view of the section to be blasted.

After a countdown on all radio channels, followed by more sirens, there was a moment of silence as onlookers studied the terrain ahead. I then heard the boom of exploding dynamite, as the ground shook to life, sending clouds of dirt into the air. After Curly gave the all-clear, life returned to normal. The night shift crews were already in pre-start meetings, learning about their tasks ahead, including the blasted area which needed to be mined.

*

After three years of living out of a holdall, the time came for me to hang up my boots. Although I'd enjoyed the experience, the constant travelling and time away from family had taken their toll. I seemed to spend more time texting Fran than chatting to her face to face. The boys were growing quickly, and I felt disconnected from their lives. My social life had also imploded, as I was rarely around for functions.

An hour after my final shift, I completed a circuit of the walking track, watching the red rocks come to life as the sun dropped towards a nearby ridgeline. I'd already said goodbye to Tim, with plans to meet again in Perth. He had mining in his blood, with no plans to try anything different.

While approaching my cabin I spotted a gecko scuttling across the mesh of my door. I crouched to take a photo and my mobile rang. The signal was weak, and the boys were singing in the background. Fran wanted to share some important news about her mum's health. As I stepped away in search of a better signal, two miners headed past, engrossed in a friendly argument about a recent footy match. Their laughter carried far on the still night air, but within minutes I was alone once more.

After saying goodnight to Fran and the boys, I headed to my cabin for the last time. Outside, I could hear the resident gecko scrambling across the hot tin roof. I fell asleep while listening to its nocturnal roaming, knowing it wouldn't be long before I was home for good.

Dreamtime

"Mad dogs and Englishmen go out in the midday sun."
– Noel Coward

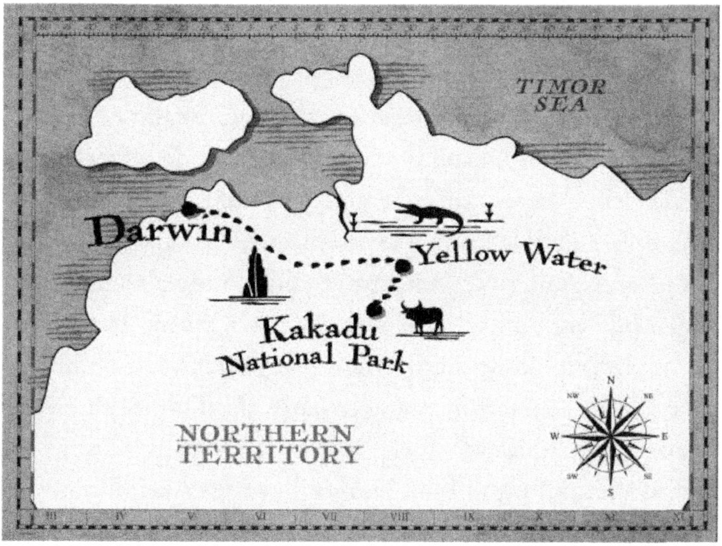

Under a perfect blue sky, the Qantas 737 touched down in Darwin. It was late November and the flight from Perth with my family had been a relaxed one, with plenty of spare seats and extra servings of in-flight meals. The number of visitors to this part of Australia dwindles between October and December, for one main reason. It is a time of oppressive heat, with no rain and high humidity. Visitors who stay too long are prone to *going troppo*.

Spotting someone who's *gone troppo* is easy. They are often white skinned, with a red neck, and no idea where they are heading as they spend useless amounts of energy running around in the midday sun. Think mad dogs, eager tourists and Englishmen. The locals, it seems, have learned to adapt. Just like those who live in warmer climes such as the Mediterranean, they seek cool places during the hottest periods to escape the humidity and sunshine. This could be their air-conditioned homes, shopping malls, the cinema or the local pub, often referred to as the watering hole!

Darwin is the capital of the Northern Territory, a vast wilderness over five times larger than the United Kingdom. The upper part is known as the Top End and is renowned for its grassland, rivers, mangroves and floodplains. In places, you will encounter crocodile-infested rivers that carve through steep gorges, millions of years old. From this ancient heartland, the rivers meander towards the Timor Sea. When it comes to the weather, the main variance throughout the year is the amount of rain. Non-indigenous Australians refer to the Top End as having two seasons. It is either very wet (the Wet), or extremely dry (the Dry).

Local Aboriginals have a different viewpoint. They observe the subtle moods and characteristics of the landscape, plants and wildlife throughout the year and believe the Northern Territory has six different seasons. According to their calendar, we were visiting during a period called *Gunumeleng*. This is when the natural world moves at a slower pace and prepares for the torrential rains, which will once again replenish the land.

By the time we touched down in Darwin, the build-up to the rainy season had already begun. A hazy band of peppered clouds lingered on the horizon, and local forecasters were predicting the dried riverbeds would be flowing by Christmas. Vast areas of savannah would then become submerged, blocking off roads and remote communities for months.

My best friend, Steve, had booked a four-week holiday from England with his family, with plans to visit Singapore and Australia during their worldwide tour. Despite the chance of torrential rain, they'd picked the Northern Territory as their first Australian location. The possibility of going troppo or getting drenched in the Wet didn't seem to faze them. This was their only opportunity to experience the Top End, and they were prepared to gamble that the rains would hold.

So, with time in short supply, the plan was simple. Both families would meet in Darwin, before heading inland to spend time in Kakadu National Park. After the trip, Steve and his family would then continue to Sydney for the next leg of their Australian tour.

We were the first to arrive in Darwin and I'd booked both families into a three-star motel along the tourist strip. All we needed now was a taxi to get us there. While we waited in air-conditioned comfort for our luggage to appear on the conveyor, I received a text message from Steve and his wife, Mel.

At that moment, they were lounging by their hotel pool, enjoying a Singapore Sling before heading to Changi Airport with their two children. It had been a few years since we'd last met, and the thought of a reunion caused me to smile as we collected our luggage and headed towards the exit. Fran was in full stride, as Noah and Sebastian ran alongside the luggage trolley, eager to set foot in the Northern Territory.

The automatic doors opened to reveal a burst of sunshine, and we waltzed full gallop into a veil of air so warm and clammy that each of us momentarily stopped in our tracks. It was only a short stroll to the taxi rank, but the humidity acted like treacle. After a few more steps, Seby hugged his mum's legs and cried out, 'Mummy, please. I'm hot and thirsty.'

Fran looked over at me, but I didn't respond. If we couldn't make it to the taxi rank without faltering, what type of adventure-family were we? Noah decided he was also suffering and called out, 'Daddy, water, please.'

I ruffled his hair and pointed to the line of travellers waiting for a ride. 'We've just spent three hours on a flight and during that time we were wined, dined, watered and entertained. The taxi rank is just ahead and I'm sure we can all make it there without falling in a heap.'

Noah turned towards his mum and repeated the words, hoping to receive a far more compassionate response. Our boys were young, just three and five years old, so I should have been far more sympathetic, and felt a niggle of guilt as we joined the taxi queue. Fran left me to ponder my actions, taking the children in search of water as I watched over our luggage. I didn't want to admit that I now regretted getting into the holiday mood by enjoying a few beers during the flight, while watching a rerun of the classic movie, *Apocalypse*

Now. Just like the jungles of Vietnam, the air felt hot and sticky with no respite to ease the pounding in my head.

Our taxi driver was a thickset, bearded man of few words. As we drove away from the airport, he mumbled about the lack of rain before turning his attention to the radio. What he lacked in conversation, he made up for with a functional air conditioner, which blasted cool air across the interior. While listening to a Beach Boys classic, we sped through Darwin's outer suburbs towards the thought of a refreshing shower, followed by a welcome dip in the pool.

The driver finally found his voice as he wrestled our luggage from the boot and pointed towards the motel doorway. 'Are you sure this is where you're staying? I haven't dropped anyone here for years.'

I checked my paperwork and gave him the thumbs up, but he was already backing away, phone to his ear, asking the caller for an address. As Fran ushered us inside, I tried remembering why the motel had grabbed my attention during the online search. Although cheap compared to others nearby, it still offered a family-friendly pool and the chance to enjoy a complimentary continental breakfast.

On closer inspection, some guests that wandered between the reception area and courtyard looked and sounded as though they were migrant families in transit to a new life in Australia. Some wore dark robes, others dashed past, eyes to the floor, avoiding any contact.

The booking website had described the bedrooms as *neat and spacious*. As the boys rushed down a gloomy corridor, fighting between them to hold the room key, they didn't seem to care where we were, as long as it had a pool.

Once inside the sparsely furnished room, I yanked open the stiff curtains and watched the walls brighten as light flooded through the windows. The walls were lined with thin cracks, creeping from the ceiling, across the width of the room and down towards the fake timber floor. To stir the clammy air, an overhead fan, controlled by two speeds, hung from the ceiling.

The first option produced a gentle whirr, which did little to disturb the trapped heat inside the four walls. The second speed proved to be far more exciting. The solitary light bulb dimmed as the fan picked up speed and revved towards maximum revolutions, its wide blades swishing noisily through the air.

To escape the mugginess, Fran suggested a dip in the pool and prepared the children for a swim. On closer inspection, the bathing area looked nothing like the stunning image that had appeared on my computer screen when making the online booking. Instead of a pool that could cater for many families, we discovered an oval plunge pool overlooked by a stack of plastic loungers.

One consolation proved to be the majestic palms, which stood to attention just outside the protective railings. They offered plenty of shade for Fran as she laid out beach towels and smeared the boys in sunscreen. As for the water, although it felt warm enough to bathe in, the colour looked milky green rather than a vibrant blue. The children didn't seem deterred and were eager to take a dip.

Instead of joining them, I decided it was time to find the nearest car hire franchise, which according to the friendly motel receptionist was only a few blocks away. As I waved goodbye, Fran passed me a bottle of water and pointed to my bald head. 'Don't forget your baseball cap.'

With a spring in my step, I called out, 'I'll be okay. It's just down the road, and the walk will clear my head!'

After navigating a dimly lit corridor, I strolled past the reception desk and bounded outside. The sudden glare from the sun took me by surprise, and for a fleeting moment I contemplated a swift U-turn to collect my sunglasses and hat. The thought vanished in an instant, knowing the car hire building was close by. I stepped away from the doorway, shielded my eyes from the sun and began searching for road signs. While getting my bearings, it soon became clear that I was the only pedestrian within view.

Every other person I could see was sitting in a car. As I walked along the empty streets, drivers glanced over before returning their stares to the road ahead. Where possible, I stayed close to buildings, to take advantage of a thin bead of shade. Only then could I study the colourful tourist map handed over by the receptionist. On closer inspection, it had no scale, and I still had a long way to go.

Instead of turning back, I cracked open the bottle of water and made my way towards the next intersection. While waiting for the lights to change, I drained the bottle, savouring every precious drop. Two rows of cars were lined up behind a faded white line, revving impatiently as I ambled past. The drivers wore sunglasses and stared straight ahead in air-conditioned nirvana, as I cast my eyes to the cobalt sky.

When I finally located the car hire franchise, a welcome breeze from the wall-mounted air conditioner whipped across my sweaty scalp. I stopped momentarily, wiped my brow and sucked in a lungful of cool air. Within the space of three steps, the temperature had dropped from an oppressive 40 degrees to a seemingly chilly 20.

As I stood by the doorway, a dark-haired girl, dressed in a navy-blue jacket and matching skirt, looked up from her computer and smiled brightly. 'G'day, mate. How can I help?'

'Water, please!' were the first words that came out of my parched mouth as I stepped towards the counter. Without a word, she swivelled 180 degrees on her office chair, walked into another room and returned with a tall glass, filled with chilled water. I drained it in one go before requesting a top-up. As my throat eased, I smiled and said thanks, hoping I now looked capable of striking a good deal. She then asked, 'Did you walk here, mate?'

I placed the empty glass down and gave a weary smile. 'I thought the afternoon stroll would do me good, after the long flight from Perth.'

She rolled her eyes and let out a chuckle. 'Most visitors jump in the hotel pool as soon as they arrive and then call us after they've cooled down. People rarely walk far at this time of the year. Are you English?'

During the trek back to the motel, the late afternoon sun continued its onslaught on my exposed scalp, and once again, cars proved they ruled over pedestrians. At each junction, they raced past, oblivious to the solitary pedestrian leaning against the traffic light pole, waiting for the green man to help him cross.

After reaching the motel, I staggered into my room, guzzled on water, closed the curtains, switched the fan to its maximum and collapsed onto the bed. The build-up to the holiday had been frantic, with too much overtime and not enough sleep. I'd finally hit the wall. For a while, I stared up at the swishing blades until my eyes began to droop. Sometime later, I was sucked into a hazy dream, where little green men called for me to join them in a sparkling pool.

I woke sluggishly to the distant sound of helicopter blades and opened my eyes to stare at the overhead fan. While stirring to life, I had a hazy flashback to a scene in *Apocalypse Now*. Just like Benjamin L. Willard, the American Army Captain in Saigon, I felt dazed, hungover and confused. Maybe I was already going troppo!

Suddenly, the door burst open and the room became flooded with bright light as someone pulled back the curtains. I sat upright just as Fran and the boys came into view, refreshed and excited after their time in the pool. Noah took one look at me, toddled over, and said, 'Daddy, why are you in bed? The pool was fun.'

Steve and his family touched down after midnight, after enjoying a few days at a luxurious stopover resort. I remained awake until their arrival, keen to rekindle a friendship that had been teetering on the brink. Steve's parting words, when I moved from England to Australia, had stayed with me for years. 'I don't do virtual friends very well. I like people I can visit each week without the need to get on an airplane! Australia is a long way away, so don't expect a visit anytime soon.'

Now he was here with his family. Steve has always been abrupt when he deems it necessary, and I've always appreciated this trait, as well as his honesty. I missed his quirky viewpoints and infectious laughter. I was also godfather to his oldest daughter, Molly, but had rarely been in touch. What kind of role model had I become?

Mel would forgive me. Wouldn't she? We'd become good friends since Steve had started dating her, and it had thrilled me to be their best man. But I was becoming a stranger now. To Molly and Daisy, I was more of a name than an actual person, my image a faint memory as the years rolled by. I could imagine the conversation on the flight to Australia, as Mel explained where the young girls were going.

Mel: 'Girls, we're nearly in Darwin. Don't forget to be polite to Uncle Ali and Aunty Fran.'

Daisy: 'Is Uncle Ali really our uncle?'

Mel: 'Well, no, but that's what you've always called him.'

Molly: 'Why did he move to Australia with Aunty Fran?'

Mel: 'They went there for an adventure after Uncle Ali lost his job.'

Daisy: 'Have they got a pet kangaroo?'

Mel: 'No, Daisy. We probably won't see any kangaroos unless we go to a wildlife park. They haven't got any pets, as far as I know.'

Daisy: 'Is Uncle Ali still bald?'

Mel: 'Of course, and probably more wrinkled than the last time we met.'

Daisy: 'Is Daddy still his friend?'

Mel: 'Yes, my dear. But your dad hasn't seen him in a few years, so it might be emotional when they meet.'

Molly: 'Does Uncle Ali still think he's funny?'

Mel: 'I guess so. Some things never change. Now let's settle down and finish the movie, as we've started to descend.'

By now, I was dressed in a singlet and shorts and had followed suit with many other guests by leaving my sandals behind. While standing barefoot in the hotel foyer, I studied my complexion in a nearby mirror and smiled wearily at the sight of the sunburnt and unshaven man staring back.

Overnight, I'd turned from a conservatively dressed suburbanite into a red-necked hillbilly. I must have nodded off by the unmanned reception desk, as I didn't hear their taxi arrive. They shuffled through the doorway, carrying rucksacks and holdalls, and then stood silently in the entrance as I rose to greet them.

As my eyes adjusted to the gloomy surroundings, I felt a rush of emotions at seeing them all. The girls had grown heaps since my last visit and it suddenly struck me that I knew so little of their lives back in England. By the time I'd come to my senses, my mind whirred with questions.

Why were they all wearing long trousers and walking boots?
Why had I booked us all into such a crappy motel?
Why had they packed so much luggage?
Why were they all staring at me?

As Steve sidestepped a discarded daypack, he shook my outstretched hand and followed up with a hug. He then stepped back while eyeing me up and down, masking a grin. 'The Australian lifestyle seems to suit you, Ali. I see you've dressed up for the occasion and know all the top places to stay in Darwin.'

Mel smiled wearily, as their two young girls sat on the floor, oblivious to my requests for high fives, begging instead for water and their beds! While the children slept, the adults sat quietly together, sharing pizzas and sipping drinks, while reminiscing about the past and catching up on gossip. Steve and I had previously enjoyed many adventures together and had always hoped our children would become close friends and share similar escapades. We were now together in the Top End of Australia, finally taking steps to make that happen.

After a few days in Darwin to experience the local sights, we collected the hired cars and then headed into the interior. Our destination was Kakadu National Park, which is roughly half the size of Switzerland. Instead of snow-capped mountains, lakes and picture-postcard villages, it has wooded savannah, floodplains and crocodile-infested rivers!

The heart of Kakadu lies 300 kilometres east of Darwin and after leaving behind the outer suburbs, we came across an expanse of red dirt, covered with hardy shrubs. Before us lay a road into no man's land–filled with rivers, gorges and vast tracts of open plains. Far on the horizon, a shimmering haze gave few clues to what lay beyond, as the tropical sun beat down on a parched landscape, waiting for the rains. After cranking the air conditioning, I called out a warning to the kids to watch out for crocodiles, snakes and kangaroos. We were heading into the wild!

We stopped soon after, to take photos of a large road sign depicting the bold outline of a kangaroo. While waving away bush flies, we noticed a series of termite mounds about 200 metres away, each one taller than a man. As we set off to investigate, the children made a dash for freedom, ignoring the calls from their concerned parents as they bounded across the baked red dirt.

'Seby, wait there for me. Where's your hat gone?'
'Molly, goodness me. Watch out for snakes.'
'Daisy, don't you dare touch anything!'
'Girls, have you put on sunscreen?'
'Noah, put your shoes back on.'

The ochre linings of each mound were pitted and battle-scarred from the onslaught of the elements. But deep inside, the termites were protected. To help insulate themselves from the sun, termites construct their homes with broad backs facing east-west and thin edges facing north-south. Their living chambers are also interlinked with vertical ventilation shafts, which create a natural air conditioner. Regardless of the outside temperature, this feat of engineering cools the core to a liveable temperature for the millions of hard-working insects inside.

The rest of the morning's journey proved uneventful, as we drove along a sealed road framed either side by an expanse of woodland. The trees and shrubs looked vibrant and green despite the lack of rain and in places we spotted creeks and rivers. Some looked dry and dusty, and others glistened with life. By lunchtime we were booked into a tourist park, complete with neat cabins, a sparkling pool and an on-site restaurant.

'Look, Daddy, a frog,' Seby called out, as we played together in the shallow end of the pool. He climbed onto my back, and I swam nearer to investigate. The amphibian was nearly as wide as my hand, with tiny warts on its dappled back, and I had a good idea this was our first encounter with a cane toad.

They were introduced into Australia by the Bureau of Sugar Experiment Stations, which was set up in 1900 by the Queensland Government. The role of the bureau was to reduce the effect of pests on cane crops, especially the larvae of native grey-backed cane beetles, which are known to destroy the roots of sugarcane. After years of trial and error with various chemicals, the bureau introduced cane toads from Hawaii in 1935.

Initially, 2,400 of these feral amphibians were released into the cane fields and since this time they have multiplied many times. Although they have enjoyed munching cane beetles and have eaten thousands, if not millions of them over the years, the story doesn't end there. Cane toads are toxic, and Australian predators are not adapted to cope with ingesting the poisonous glands that protrude from their skin.

They may look like easy prey, but there has been a massive reduction in goanna and snake populations in areas inhabited by cane toads. There is worse news to come as they have a natural tendency to travel and have hopped across Queensland, New South Wales and many parts of the Northern Territory.

They now number 200 million and are seemingly unstoppable as they continue to impact the environment while migrating further west and south. As for the native grey-backed cane beetle, they are still considered a pest, but the Bureau of Sugar Experiment Stations is unusually quiet about the topic these days!

I picked up the toad by one of its meaty legs, and together with Seby, we walked across a manicured lawn towards the camp restaurant. Inside, a few workers were enjoying cool drinks during their break. While crossing the floor, I held up the specimen and said, 'Excuse me, but my young lad found this in the pool. I think it's a cane toad.'

Their conversation ceased as they studied the warty creature dangling from my fingers. One man stood, adjusted his wide-brimmed hat and came closer to investigate. He had piercing blue eyes, a weathered face, and the steady gait of someone in charge. As he approached, he took one look at the creature and said in a slow drawl, 'Yes, mate. That's a cane toad. Well spotted!'

He then kneeled and looked at Seby. 'Hey young fellow, do you like Australian wildlife?'

Seby nodded, but was unusually quiet, and squeezed my free hand with his. The man ruffled Seby's fair hair, stood upright and said, 'Well I'm glad, and so do I. This here is a cane toad and in Kakadu we hate them with a vengeance. They kill our wildlife, and with a destructive creature like this, there's just one thing to do. Now, listen to me and close your eyes if you don't like the sight of blood.'

He then took the toad and hurled it against a wall with such ferocity that it splattered hard, fell to the floor and lay still. He then tossed it into an outside bin, before returning to his drink. Just before we left, he gave some advice. 'If you see any more of those feral things during your stay, feel free to do the same.'

Seby couldn't wait to tell the other children about the new game of cane toad bashing, and they spent the rest of the afternoon searching for them in the confines of the lawn and pool area. I gave a bounty for each one, and a few hours later, Australia only had 199,999,997 left to exterminate.

The following morning, we drove towards South Alligator River, a vast, aquatic wilderness, filled with billabongs, floodplains and swamps. We parked close to the community of Jabiru and spent a few lazy hours cruising along Yellow Water Billabong, home to a prolific number of bird species. It is also teeming with crocodiles!

Our river guide had one golden rule, which we all agreed to follow. 'Keep all body parts in the boat unless you want to be chomped by a croc!'

As we glided through the pristine waters, spotting crocs from the safety of the boat became an easy pastime. Some floated near the edge of the river, lying perfectly still, with just their steely eyes and speckled snouts showing above the waterline. Most, it seemed, were basking in the sunshine along the riverbank. Overhead, magpie geese and whistling ducks flew in formation, while great egrets foraged in the shallow waters, probing for food amongst a carpet of blue lilies.

With the boat tour over, it was time to meet our Aboriginal guide, Patsy, one of the last remaining hunter-gatherers in Australia. She collaborates with a travel organisation called Animal Tracks, to take visitors on tours across her tribal land while sharing her knowledge about bush tucker and the environment. *Bush tucker* is the term that Australians use for food found in the wild. Bush means wilderness, and tucker is the Australian slang for food.

Bush tucker skills are becoming rare, as Aboriginals abandon their traditional way of life. Most have adopted a hybrid lifestyle where they still live together in family communities but crave western world indulgences. Indigenous populations across the world have struggled when faced with these cultural changes, and Aboriginals are no different.

At midday we met Rachael, the representative from Animal Tracks. After brief introductions with other passengers, Rachael shared that she'd once been a Kakadu park ranger. She also explained that Patsy was a traditional owner of the land and had lived in the Northern Territory all her life, much of the time as a nomad.

This news sparked an interest among most passengers, which led to a series of questions about the wildlife and weather, including the dark clouds forming on the horizon. Rachael dismissed the idea of rain, at least for a day or two, but let slip that the tourist season would soon come to an end.

With the talking over, we boarded a four-wheel-drive truck and headed into the bush to meet Patsy. While we bounced in the back, Rachael informed us about the importance of Kakadu, including its status as being dual listed by UNESCO for its outstanding natural and cultural values.

Thirty minutes later we turned onto a gravel road surrounded by greenery, with a scattering of dwellings hidden behind trees. Patsy was standing by the roadside, dressed in a long green skirt, matching top and training shoes. She joined Rachael up front, turning around to greet us as she hopped on board. Her hair was a wild frizz of golden-yellow and her dark skin had a healthy glow. As Rachael drove us towards Kakadu Buffalo farm reserve, Patsy joined her in small talk while the passengers glugged water and exchanged travel stories within the close confines of the rear seats.

After disembarking, I took a few steps away from the excited children to study Patsy's homeland. The air crackled with the sound of droning insects, and in the nearby trees, flocks of noisy waterbirds sheltered from the sun. The grassland nearby looked firm, but in the distance, isolated pockets were covered in a veneer of still water, fringed by lilies and colourful wildflowers.

Patsy emerged from the rear of the truck and handed each of us a wooden pole. As the group fell silent, she held her pole up and called for attention. 'I use this for finding long-necked turtles, as they're hibernating in the mud. Watch me first and you'll soon learn.'

The children ran by her side as she strode across the meadow, then found a suitable location at the base of a paperbark tree. She prodded the pole into the mud until the tip had sunk knee deep. Just as quickly, she pulled it out and stabbed at another area close by. One child began talking but was hushed by a parent as Patsy stepped forward to probe elsewhere. It took several attempts until she got lucky. In the silence, each of us heard a submerged shell being tapped by her pole.

She then bent down, plunged her hands into the moist earth and scooped out a long-necked turtle. The waking creature was placed into a hessian bag, as Patsy urged us to continue searching. The children ran towards the boggiest patch and were soon plastered in a sheen of black mud, as they hunted for their dinner. Within 30 minutes, the group had located two more turtles and Patsy called a halt. 'That is enough,' she announced, with quiet authority. 'We must only take what we need.'

Rachael and Patsy worked well together, and as we traversed the landscape, stopping to forage for herbs and paperbark, they informed us about the abundance of bush tucker in the region. Patsy had already caught and killed two magpie geese before we'd collected her. They were now in a hessian bag, waiting to be plucked.

Our last jaunt involved a hunt for file snakes, in a billabong at the edge of the reserve. They struggle to move on land because of their loose skin, and when Patsy plucked a metre-long, spear-wide reptile from the water and placed it onto the grass, it lay sluggishly on the bank. She then turned towards the group and said, 'Okay. I need a volunteer to help me prepare the snake.'

Fran's hand shot up in an instant. 'Yes, I'll do it.'

Patsy picked up the snake by its tail and stepped closer. 'No worries. All you do is take the head in your mouth and crunch down hard.'

Although Fran's hand dropped away, she still moved forward to collect the snake. Before reaching out, she said, 'I might try, but is it poisonous?'

'No, lady. Don't worry. I will show you how it's done. But before we kill the snake, I have one question for you all. Do we have enough food already?'

The group fell silent for a few moments, but from the edge of the billabong, Molly called out, 'I think we have plenty already, so please let it go.'

After a murmur of agreement, Patsy returned the snake to the water and declared an end to the hunting trip! By now, the sun had lost its edge, and the harsh light from earlier had been replaced by a soft radiance, which brushed the treetops and turned the grassland into a swathe of amber gold. During the last hour of daylight, a campfire was lit, and while we prepared dinner, a herd of water buffalo appeared from the bush.

Weighing up to a tonne and standing close to two metres at the shoulder, they are a formidable sight. These feral animals were introduced in the 1800s from Indonesia, to supply meat to remote northern settlements. Just like cane toads, they have flourished in the Northern Territory, but are now being culled because of their destructive impact on the environment. The list against them is long, including their ability to cause soil erosion and water contamination. They also have an insatiable appetite for local grasses meant for native animals.

Unlike cane toads, which can be squashed or bashed on the head, water buffalo culling requires far more firepower, involving helicopters and snipers! The ones close to our camp didn't look threatening, despite their wide horns. They roamed across the adjoining paddock, skirted a band of woodland and stopped to graze.

As they crossed our line of sight, Patsy pulled a turtle from her bag and handed it to Steve. He stood for a moment, unsure of what to do, and caressed its long neck while his family watched. It was a classic setting, with the sun dropping low on the horizon, outlining the wide horns of the far-away buffalo.

Patsy's words of wisdom soon broke the serenity. 'You gonna stroke it or kill it, mister? Your family is hungry. Break its neck so we can roast it!'

As Steve grappled with the wriggling creature, his two children looked on in amazement. They were now smeared in dried mud, and throughout the afternoon hadn't complained once about the heat, mosquitos or lack of toilets. Two days earlier, Mel had been sipping cocktails in Singapore. Now she was sitting in the red dirt, humming a Scottish ballad while plucking feathers from dead geese. At the edge of our camp, Noah and Seby were enjoying spear-throwing lessons from Rachael, while Fran prepared fresh herbs for dinner.

The seasoned meat was then covered in paperbark and roasted along the edge of the fireplace. Nothing was wasted, as we silently devoured the succulent geese, turtle and sweet potatoes. With dinner complete, Patsy promised a nutritional snack for dessert and led us to a line of paperbark trees at the edge of camp. After gently peeling a section of bark from the base of the first tree, she revealed a scattering of green ants.

With deft fingers, she plucked a few insects to create a thumb-sized morsel. As the children watched, she popped the ants into her mouth. After a quick chew, followed by a gulp and a smile, she then said, 'They're just like lemons. Now you try.'

The children were keen, picking off ants between fits of giggles, as the tiny creatures crawled across fingers, hands and faces. The trick was to collect enough to create a slightly crushed ball, to ensure you had no rogue ants roaming alone in your mouth. Each morsel delivered a sharp burst of zingy lemon, high in vitamin C and instantly addictive.

From far away, Rachael announced it was time to leave, and as we headed towards the truck, I realised that Noah was missing. I quickly studied the distant buffalo for signs of activity, then ran towards the dampened fireplace and searched the camp. Fran had already located him and called me over to watch his activities.

He'd gone in search of more dessert and was standing by a nearby tree trunk, murmuring to himself while picking off green ants. His blonde curly hair was matted with mud and his clothes were now unrecognisable, but he, like all the visitors, had learned so much in one short day.

Far on the horizon, dark clouds were forming, their wispy edges blushed from the setting sun. As the weary group boarded the truck for the return journey, I heard Patsy talking with Rachael. 'The rains are coming. I think this will be our last week of the tourist season.'

Within 48 hours, Steve and his family departed for Sydney. The skies above Darwin Airport were dark and foreboding, and I watched from the departure lounge as swirling clouds swallowed their plane. They were now in search of their next adventure with plans to climb Sydney Harbour Bridge, visit family and take surfing lessons at Bondi Beach. Our flight would take us south to Perth, followed by a three-hour drive home.

Two weeks later, they arrived at our front door and we finally had them to ourselves. They'd woken that morning on the east coast, flown across the country, hired a car and were now in the southwest of Australia. After a hectic few weeks, my initial fears for them had come true. They looked exhausted.

While they'd been gallivanting, Fran and I had planned many day trips to show off our part of the world, to help give them an insight into our daily lives. Fran had scrubbed the house while I worked on the alfresco and booked friends around for social gatherings. The weather looked inviting, with unbroken sunshine forecast for the week ahead. The outside fridge brimmed with fresh juices for the girls, a range of drinks for Mel and locally brewed ales for Steve. We were ready to enjoy balmy evenings under the stars, while listening to their Australian adventures and playing games with the children.

While I gave them an impromptu house tour, pointing out where to find snacks, mosquito repellent and sunscreen, Steve remained unusually quiet. The girls had disappeared, running off with the boys to check out the bunk beds, while Fran and Mel were already comparing décor and sipping wine.

I led Steve into the back garden, hoping he'd comment on the decking area, recently oiled and now decorated with an array of tropical plants housed in terracotta pots. I'd picked one area to showcase a selection of knick-knacks from my global travels, including an abstract mural from Zimbabwe and a mining lantern from the southern highlands of Bolivia. Pride of place was a framed photo of the two of us, proudly holding up ice axes while clad in thick fleeces and ski masks. We were standing on the summit of Mont Blanc, 4,809 metres above sea level.

But he brushed past the artefacts without a second glance, his eyes finding our striped hammock swaying in the warm summer breeze. He dropped his daypack onto the grass, kicked off his sandals and eased into the hammock, sighing softly as his long legs curled around the sides. For a few seconds there was silence, and then he said, 'I know you'll have heaps of things planned for us. Wineries, I'm guessing, and deep-sea fishing, plus a chance to meet your new mates.'

I had the wish-list folded in my pocket, ready to show him, but something told me to keep it there. 'To tell you the truth,' he began, 'we're worn out from travelling. All I want to do is relax at the beach, read a book and spend time in the hammock with a few cold beers. We've seen every alcove and beach in Sydney, but always seemed to drive past them instead of lying on them. I'm sure the wineries around here are amazing, but I'm tired of day trips. I'm not bothered about deep-sea fishing or travelling too far.'

I understood his wishes. Australia is a massive country, and too many travellers try to skim across vast distances within a short period to experience the main sights. I left him swaying, grabbed two cold beers and placed the wish-list in a drawer.

Their last days in Australia were relaxed and simple. We stayed local, embracing the beaches, coves, coastal walks and cafes. Steve also got plenty of time to laze in the hammock! Throughout these idle days, we talked a lot. About dreams, aspirations, future travels, and coming to terms with living nineteen hours' flight time from best friends. We made plans to stay in touch with video calls and regular email updates, and sat together by the front porch most evenings, binoculars poised for signs of bird life or kangaroos in the adjacent wetlands.

On their last morning, I launched my four-metre aluminium boat into the clear, pristine waters of Geographe Bay. The ocean resembled a millpond, with barely a ripple on the horizon. All morning we explored the bay, fishing for herring, skipjack and squid. Mel and the girls dropped crab pots into the water, and then shrieked with delight as they pulled two large crustaceans from the depths, their bright blue pincers gnashing in defence.

After trawling the waters and trying different spots, we soon had enough to prepare chilli crab, fried squid and a taste of herring. As the sun rose higher, a southerly breeze stirred the water, and sailboats appeared on the scene, signalling a racing event across the bay. It was time to head home for our final barbeque.

As I throttled the outboard, the boat changed pitch and skimmed across the water. Steve lay upfront, tanned and relaxed, his long arms dangling over the sides. We sped across the bay, past a lone kayaker and family-sized fishing boats, then headed towards the town jetty, a 1.8 kilometre timber-piled structure that juts proudly into the Indian Ocean. Anglers were dotted along its length, each with their own secret spot, as they waited patiently for a bite. I turned the tiller and sped parallel with the jetty, keeping far from fishing lines while aiming for shore.

Just off our bow, a dolphin surfaced, its dorsal fin carving through the water. As the beach drew nearer, I eased off the revs, and the boat slowed. Steve turned away from the water and glanced over towards me, his face a beaming smile. As I cut the engine and let the boat glide towards the sand, he said, 'On a day like today, I understand why you live in Australia.'

House of Fun

"I do love cricket. It's so very English."
– Sarah Bernhardt

Every two years, cricket fans get the chance to watch a five match test series between Australia and England, known as *The Ashes*. The name is derived from an epitaph, printed by a newspaper called *The Sporting Times*, in August 1882. Australia had just won their first game on English soil, resulting in an outpouring of shock and emotion from the British public. The epitaph read:

An affectionate remembrance of English Cricket, which died at The Oval on 29th August 1882. Deeply lamented by a large circle of sorrowing friends and acquaintances. R.I.P. N.B. The body will be cremated and the ashes taken to Australia.

When the English team next visited Australia, they were presented with a red glazed pottery urn, just over four inches tall, supposedly holding the ashes of a single wicket bail. It is this urn that the teams now play for each time they meet.

*

Sydney is a dream location to visit, so when the opportunity came to travel from Perth to watch the final Ashes cricket test of the series, I didn't need too much convincing. I hadn't envisaged that the England cricket team would be four-nil down by the time I reached Sydney, but as the taxi dropped my two friends and me outside the historic cricket stadium, there was little evidence from the carnival atmosphere that a whitewash was looming.

Bright sunshine forced us to abandon our seats in favour of the spectator's bar, and while queuing for refreshments I joined in with the banter as Australian and English fans traded jokes and discussed the play so far. From afar, I could see a mass of red-and-white, signalling the location of a band of English supporters, seated in the glaring sunshine.

Over the years, some of these supporters have formed a movement called the Barmy Army. This passionate group of English cricket fans love to travel around the world to watch their team in action. During this time, they've gained fame for their carefree demeanour, coupled with their catchy songs and witty verses which are performed during matches. The majority of their lyrics are directed towards the rival team or their fans. It's done in jest, and as part of their repertoire they also have a seasoned trumpet player to add a little panache and harmony when the need arises.

The Australian fans were sitting close by, soaking up the sunshine and enjoying every moment of the cricket. Their team had won the last four tests and were in pole position to win the series outright. Some fans wore Mexican sombrero hats and others were dressed in canary-yellow shirts. But most seemed happy to wear the traditional Aussie attire of surfing shorts and cotton singlets.

While I watched from the shade, two English supporters stood up. Both wore white cricket shirts, decorated with a logo depicting three lions. As the match continued, they turned to face the Australian fans and belted out a catchy song (to the tune of 'Yellow Submarine' by The Beatles).

Within a few seconds, hundreds of fans joined in, as they pointed towards the Australian spectators.

'*You all live in a convict colony, a convict colony, a convict colony...*'

As the song finished, the English followers burst into applause. After the noise had died down, a nearby group of Australian supporters stood to face the Barmy Army. In raised voices, they hollered out the score, reminding the English fans their team was getting thrashed. One passionate fan went a stage further, raising his plastic glass of beer high while waiting for silence. He was short and stocky, with a bushy beard and trimmed moustache. His frothy ale swilled as he called out the three words his friends were waiting to hear. '*Aussie, Aussie, Aussie!*'

Those around him responded to the war cry, singing the next line with gusto as the words, '*Oi, Oi, Oi,*' resounded across the stadium. The remainder of the song was over in seconds and went something like this.

'Aussie, Aussie, Aussie!'
'Oi, Oi, Oi!'
'Aussie!'
'Oi!'
'Aussie!'
'Oi!'

The final two lines were delivered at speed, as the man hollered out, '*Aussie, Aussie, Aussie!*' and waited for the rousing reply. It came a split second later, sang by hundreds of Australian fans, now on their feet, gesturing to the English supporters as the words poured out. *'Aussie, Aussie, Aussie! Oi, Oi, Oi!'*

In a final act, the bearded cheerleader sculled his beer and sat back down, smiling and laughing while receiving pats on the back from nearby friends.

Not wanting to be outdone, the English supporters replied. A blonde-haired man, dressed as a medieval knight, stood tall and raised his hands high. He then cleared his throat and sang. Just like earlier, within a few seconds, those around him joined in.

'*We are the England–the mighty, mighty, England–we are the army–the barmy, barmy, army.*'

From what I could see of the scoreboard, this particular England team didn't seem to be mighty in any way. Despite the score, the English supporters were still determined to enjoy their time away from home. Throughout the first day, I chatted with fellow Brits as they watched from the shade or stood in line for a beer. Many had made the long-haul trip from England and this was their trip of a lifetime, regardless of the result.

Others had travelled interstate, with Australia now their new home. As the conversations flowed, I realised that those who had emigrated from England to Australia were the ones most likely to be wearing sports tops associated with their hometown in the UK. One group had travelled together from Melbourne and although they had a common purpose to support the England cricket team, they each wore different club shirts. Two of them were Liverpool fans, one supported Arsenal and another wore their Leicester rugby top with pride.

I understood why they wanted to wear their club shirts. It's about feeling part of something, although they now live on the other side of the world. Sydney seemed to be the most popular destination for those on a working-holiday visa and the travellers I spoke to were lapping up the experience of living half a world away.

Each evening, the trendy back streets reverberated with lively chants as the English supporters staked their claim to quayside bars, brushing away all thoughts of a five-nil defeat. As the days unfolded, the runs against the English team continued to grow.

By the morning of day four, I thought about all the popular tourist sites that I'd missed out on, while watching them struggle to get a decent run rate. Just after lunch, I made my excuses, dashed outside the grounds and hailed the nearest taxi. A short while later, I was standing alongside Circular Quay, grinning in anticipation at the thought of taking a stroll across Sydney Harbour Bridge.

It had been many years since my last visit to the bridge, when I'd climbed to the 134-metre summit with my sister, Alice. But this time I would not be paying hundreds of dollars for the privilege of climbing to the top as part of an organised climb. Instead, I would walk across the bridge for free, along the eastern footpath, just like hundreds of people do every day.

From Circular Quay I joined locals and tourists on board one of the ferries, and within minutes all thoughts of the latest cricket score diminished as we passed within metres of Sydney Opera House, its white-sailed roof gleaming in the afternoon sunshine. I disembarked at Luna Park and watched holidaymakers walk through the open mouth of a giant, rosy-cheeked clown, towards the fair rides and sideshows. There was no need for me to visit the House of Fun, as I knew there would be plenty of comical antics that afternoon at the cricket ground, both on and off the field. The famous bridge, with its huge buttress and formidable steel columns rising from the choppy waters, now dominated the skyline.

From Luna Park I headed towards Milsons Point, leaving behind the sound of children's laughter as I searched for the paved steps that led onto the bridge. I'd envisaged the walkway to be a local secret, but this myth was quickly dispelled by the realisation that visitors from across the world had already discovered the budget solution to awe-inspiring views. Amongst the steady flow of power walkers, joggers, transient office workers and those enjoying a leisurely stroll, I heard accents from around the world.

As they passed by, I gazed through the safety railings at the expansive views of Sydney Harbour and the Opera House. On the other side of the city, I sensed the English cricketers were plunging towards a 5-0 defeat and no amount of luck would save them. My phone beeped and then displayed the latest score. Another English wicket had just fallen. Far below, a cargo ship moved across the bay, leaving behind a creamy swirl in its wake.

Near the end of the path, I stopped to look up and caught sight of those who had paid for the experience of climbing in the rafters. The group was stretched out, moving towards the top. Soon they'd be standing at the peak, their ant-like silhouettes standing proud against the bright sky. I turned my gaze away and strode towards the end of the walkway, eager for a celebratory beer. Within two streets, I found a corner pub and took a seat at the bar.

Most of the clientele were outside, enjoying the sunshine, which meant I had the wide-screen TV to myself. Partway through my first beer, another wicket tumbled. While ordering a second drink, I heard a cheer from the barman. 'Come on Australia. They're dropping like flies!'

The TV replay showed an English batsman walking from the field, his head lowered in defeat. I left my unfinished beer on the bar, hailed a taxi and headed back to the ground. Once inside, I inched through the packed arena, drawn towards the red-and-white banners of the Barmy Army. Despite their team's imminent collapse, the supporters sang and chanted, until the final wicket remained.

I once read that the orchestra continued to play as the stricken *Titanic* began to tilt, before plunging into the icy waters of the Atlantic Ocean. Maybe it's an English trait, to stare down disaster with a calming tune. In the last few seconds, a hush descended over the cricket ground. Something was happening. You could feel the tension amongst the testosterone and sweat. Somewhere amidst the fluttering of Saint George's flags, a lone trumpet player came to life.

As the melodic tone of 'Jerusalem' carried across the ground, I heard the sound of willow on leather. The ball spun into the clear sky, but there wasn't enough weight to carry it far. In a befitting moment, the Australian captain, Michael Clarke, plucked it from the air with assured confidence. The

Australian supporters leapt as one, their roars of applause drowning out the stirring sounds of the trumpet. The Ashes were over.

In the Summertime

"Those who don't jump will never fly."
– Leena Ahmad Almashat

During my childhood, many summer holidays were spent running amok in the green hills of Donegal. I still remember joining forces with my Irish cousins to help local farmers rake hay into giant haystacks, far taller than the ruddy faced men in flat caps giving guidance between jokes and stories. With so many distractions, including friendly donkeys in an adjacent field on the lookout for carrots or a back scratch, our band of mischievous young helpers rarely worked up a sweat.

As a reward for our efforts, we'd get a few coins to spend in town later that evening, either on chips or a fizzy drink while at the children's disco. Those fun days are a fond memory, especially as I now live half a world away, in the southwest of Australia.

Busselton is not renowned for its hills or donkeys and although there are surrounding farms, most paddocks seem to wither by mid-summer. Instead of misty mountain tops, the seaside town has other attractions, including summer sunshine, golden beaches, a protected bay and one of the longest jetties in the world.

Many visitors are lured to the region each summer, either to swim, fish or play in the warm, clear waters of the Indian Ocean. The jetty attracts hundreds of thousands of holidaymakers each year, many from overseas, and the numbers continue to rise. Some are drawn to the underwater observatory at the end of the jetty, others for the chance to walk along its length for nearly two kilometres, stopping to watch dolphins or to chat with those throwing a fishing line into the water.

It was during one of those lazy summer days I found myself on the foreshore, searching for shade amongst the fig trees while Fran applied sunscreen onto our two boys, Noah and Sebastian. As they wriggled and complained, eager to get into the water, their cousins, Oliver and Eve, stood nearby while rubbing colourful stripes of zinc across their youthful faces.

For a while I joined them in the water, playing games with a ball, as toddlers splashed in the shallows, their watchful mothers standing ankle deep in the ocean, just an arm's reach away. Later, we enjoyed takeaway fish and chips while stretched out on a grassy bank, listening to the squawk of greedy gulls compete with the sounds of laughter from a beachside playground.

It was just after lunch when the children stirred to life, although this time they were not interested in the beach. Instead, they set off towards the jumping platform, located 100 metres along the jetty. Fran followed discreetly, her eyes peeled for Sebastian, our youngest, as the four cousins strolled past the jetty entrance and Interpretive Centre, designed to replicate a row of sea-blue beach huts.

I stayed further back, navigating my way across the rail track that stretches all the way to the end of the jetty. The bright red train was nowhere to be seen, meaning it was at the far end after dropping off passengers outside the underwater observatory.

While approaching the jumping platform, I spotted a group of tanned teenagers, some dripping wet from recent jumps and others bone dry, staring over a wooden railing, calling to friends in the water. For a while, I stood nearby and listened to excited conversations as youngsters encouraged each other to leap. For some, this would be their first jetty jump. A rite of passage, for all that live and holiday in Busselton.

The platform was filled with a group of teenage boys, high on testosterone, as they attempted flamboyant star jumps and frolicked in the water after each leap. While they swam back to shore, Oliver, Eve and Noah claimed their spot on the two-metre-wide platform, edging closer until their toes gripped the edge. This was to be their first ever jump, and I felt a surge of pride as Oliver, the oldest, called out, 'Okay, we can do this.'

Noah was next to speak, his brave voice carrying far. 'I'm not scared one bit.'

'Let's hold hands and just jump,' suggested Eve, her blue eyes ablaze as a crowd formed behind them. She was grinning with anticipation and showed little sign of fear. For a few seconds, they stood and gazed into the water.

I don't know which child moved first, but as a trio they leapt from the safety of the jetty and launched themselves into the air, their excited shrills reaching far across the bay as they splashed into the ocean. Within seconds, they surfaced and climbed the metal steps, eager to jump again.

The last to jump was Sebastian, the youngest cousin, just eight years of age, his freckled cheeks turning pink from the sun. He'd watched from the safety of the railing, but as they called him forward, Fran released his hand and ruffled his hair. After standing on the edge, he waited for the countdown from his cousins and jumped solo, with arms straight and mouth closed.

Holiday memories are rarely found in shopping malls or on computer games. They often occur when surrounded by friends or family, enjoying the outdoors. In years to come, the cousins will forget many things during their busy lives.

But somehow, I think they will always remember the endless summer when they first jumped off Busselton jetty into the Indian Ocean.

Sunshine on my Shoulders

"Go and sleep on a hill and go jump in a river before breakfast."
– Alastair Humphreys

'So, Ali, what's it like to live in Australia?'

The question came from my cousin, Charlie, as we stood side by side, knee-deep in an estuary, both dressed in bright yellow waders. Before us lay stacks of oyster beds, ready to be harvested from Loughros Beg Bay and sent to market.

While waiting for a reply he reached down, plucked an oyster from one of the mesh sacks, split the shell with a blade and offered me the half that contained the wild, gamey meat. As expected, it slid down easily, revealing a myriad of earthy flavours, with the essence of peat, sweet water and a hint of sea salt. I then nodded in appreciation, as Charlie explained the timely process of farming oysters in the fertile waters of the Atlantic Ocean.

My two children were close by, happily digging in the sand for cockles, along with Fran. A few days earlier we'd left behind a winter in the southwest of Australia, with its squally showers and cool nights, in exchange for four weeks of a European summer. Now we were in the wilds of Donegal, in the northwest of Ireland, at the start of our long-anticipated family holiday.

As we made our way back to the beach, I pondered Charlie's question and gave the most honest answer I could muster. 'Australia is a great place to live, but I wish it was a little nearer to all of my family.'

He grinned widely and said, 'I see the boys are getting big now. Why don't you stay for the whole of summer? Noah can learn to drive a tractor, and Seby looks like he is a natural at finding cockles.'

The thought of spending July and August in Donegal sounded idyllic. I'd spent many happy times there over the years and yearned for my children to have similar memories. But we were on a tight deadline to see other parts of Europe as well, and I only had so much time off before returning to work.

We took up Charlie's offer of tractor driving though, and the following morning Noah found himself seated high and dry, surrounded by rows of oyster beds, standing proud against the retreating tide. After a series of instructions, he tentatively took control of the tractor and steered it between each row. Soon, the trailer he towed was filled with sacks of oysters, as Charlie and his work crew laboured under the welcome sunshine.

Ten days later we were in England, enjoying valuable time with other family members. We took day trips to castles, theme parks and seaside resorts. We even enjoyed a ploughman's lunch, while sitting in the beer garden of Ye Olde Fighting Cocks, reputed to be the oldest pub in England. Later that day we played hide and seek with the children, in a field of ripening wheat.

Finally, we flew to the Greek island of Zakynthos for a week of guaranteed sunshine, along with the chance to embrace its culture and ancient history. Then, within the blink of an eye, we were back in Australia and the entire trip had seemed like a dream.

Sometime later, I injured my shoulder while playing sport, which resulted in surgery and months of rehabilitation. While convalescing, I wallowed in memories of our overseas family holiday, months before. It was Fran that pulled me to my senses. Europe was now in mid-winter, while Australia basked in summer sunshine. I could either lie in bed, complaining of a sore shoulder while thinking about faraway friends and family, or I could embrace the place in which I lived.

That afternoon, while browsing the internet, I discovered a book called *Micro Adventures*, by the British explorer Alastair Humphreys. The premise, I learned, was that you don't always have to travel far to enjoy an adventure. Often, there are adventurous options within reach, but for many reasons we overlook them.

This was true for me. I was living close to the Indian Ocean, and across from my front door were extensive wetlands, teeming with wildlife. As my shoulder healed, I looked at the places nearby through fresh eyes. My hometown has the longest timber-piled jetty in the Southern Hemisphere, measuring nearly two kilometres. Although now a major tourist destination, it has weathered many storms over the years.

Originally built to gain access to moored ships in the shallow waters of Geographe Bay, the jetty has been extended and upgraded many times since its inception in 1865. Goods such as whale oil were unloaded at the jetty, whilst timber and dairy produce were in high demand as exports.

Horse-drawn carts were used on the jetty for generations until the introduction of a train line in 1911. The last commercial vessel docked in 1971, and within a year, the jetty was closed as a shipping port.

Due to the high maintenance costs for its upkeep and the risk of becoming a navigational hazard, plans were made for the jetty's demolition. This led to an outcry from the community and the formation of a group called *Save Our Jetty*. During a meeting in 1976, the seeds were sown for an underwater observatory at the end of the jetty, to help raise its profile while providing a long-term income from visitors.

Two years later, the southwest was pounded by Cyclone Alby, with wind speeds reaching 150 kilometres per hour during its brief and destructive lifetime. The results were catastrophic, with the loss of lives, flooding, and powerful tidal surges that wiped out the first 700 metres of the oldest stretch of jetty, including the diving and swimming platforms. Thankfully, this section was a spur to the aptly named 'skeleton jetty,' which meant access could still be gained from the foreshore.

Once again, the community rallied, led in part by John Bussell, a descendent of the first family to settle in the Busselton region. In 1979, John embarked on an epic journey, walking up and down the length of the jetty for ten days. Throughout this time, he completed 151 laps, covering 579 kilometres, while raising over $5,500. Others in the community were inspired by John's efforts, resulting in many more fundraising activities to help rebuild the jetty, including the addition of an underwater observatory.

These plans were nearly scuttled in December 1999, as an overnight fire ripped through 70 metres of the jetty. To help save the end section, emergency crews and volunteer firefighters were forced to chainsaw burning timbers and let them fall into the ocean.

These inspiring efforts have been rewarded, with extensive renovations and an injection of funds to help build a world class attraction. The funds have come from many sources, including community led initiatives, the introduction of an entrance fee and support from the shire and state government.

Nowadays, the jetty attracts over six hundred thousand visitors each year, making it a major draw card in the south-west of Australia. You can walk along it, fish from it, jump from it, snorkel or scuba dive in the waters below it, and even take a train to an underwater observatory at the end.

Seals, dolphins and sharks have been spotted through the observatory windows, plus octopus and schools of herring. In fact, there are over 300 individual marine species to be found, including subtropical corals and sponges. The environment surrounding the observatory has been declared a marine sanctuary and plans are being drawn up for the chance to wine and dine while watching the undersea life.

Millions of dollars are being invested into making the jetty one of the most iconic attractions in Australia. This includes an underwater sculpture and artificial reef trail at the northern end of the jetty, designed to create a wonderland for divers, snorkellers and swimmers. The 13 sculptures will also provide habitat for sea life, with a range of designs including a 10-metre southern right whale and a three-metre seahorse, both constructed from mild steel.

During the last days of summer, I decided to paddle around the jetty. I could have picked early morning, when the wind is often the lightest, but opted instead for dusk. With luck, I'd witness a fiery sunset and be back on the beach before nightfall.

I arrived at the foreshore with the sun to my left, dropping slowly towards the low-lying hills of Cape Naturaliste. A lighthouse is positioned at the tip of the headland, but was yet to turn on its powerful beam. With help from a pedestrian, I placed my kayak onto the beach and dragged it through the warm sand towards the water's edge. Most holidaymakers were relaxing on beach towels, and one group was already setting themselves up for sundowners, with wine, beer, cheese and crackers being laid across a tartan blanket.

Toddlers picked shells from the sand, as I steadied the kayak in the water and sat upright, paddle in hand, in readiness for my micro-adventure. I started from the right-hand side of the jetty, waved farewell to the watching children and pushed away from the shore. The surrounding water looked to be a kaleidoscope of rich blues and turquoise green, stretching towards the horizon.

Within seconds, I spotted a stingray, gliding through the shallows in search of prey, including scraps of fishing bait and baby crabs. The kayak carved through the water as I paddled towards a designated jumping platform, where a group of children now stood. They'd probably been playing there for hours, coaxing each other to attempt somersaults and star jumps into the ocean. During the last minutes of daylight, they huddled together, their gangly shapes silhouetted by the setting sun.

As I paddled below them, a lone jumper broke from the group and leapt from the jetty. While in mid-air, he straightened his legs and kept his arms by his side. After plunging into the water, he surfaced with a smile and called for his friends to follow. I wanted to stay and watch the others, but still had far to travel in the fading light.

The clouds came to life just as I neared the end of the jetty, turning crimson red as I made my way past the underwater observatory and marine sanctuary. As I reached the end, nearly two kilometres from shore, the lighthouse on the faraway hills caught my attention, its narrow beam competing with the last of the sunlight. I brushed past the last wooden column, noting the swathe of barnacles clinging to the weathered timber. After a few more strokes of the paddle, I made a turn for home!

The jetty was now to my left, with small, feisty waves breaking across the bow of the kayak, causing me to paddle harder to gain momentum as a cool breeze brushed my face. The sight of a fishing line being cast from the jetty let me know I wasn't alone. I had no idea if the angler knew I was three metres below them, gritting my teeth as my injured shoulder complained.

The sun turned blood red and plunged below Cape Naturaliste, leaving behind the fiery sunset I'd hoped for. It was then that I remembered the local newspaper headline, about a recent sighting of a great white shark, near the end of the jetty. A shiver ran through me, which I put down to the stiff breeze coming straight from shore.

While halfway back, a dark shape crossed my bow, just below the waterline. It could have been seaweed, a resident stingray, or shadows cast by my imagination. My heart began pounding and, without thought, I turned to search the surrounding water. The sudden motion pitched the kayak, causing me to smack the water with the side of the paddle blade. As the kayak steadied, a dorsal fin broke the surface, slicing through the water with ease.

By the time I blinked away the ocean spray, the fin had vanished. My stomach knotted as I paddled hard towards shore, convincing myself it was a dolphin, but afraid that it wasn't. I focused on the faraway street lights and pumped my arms, knowing that each paddle stroke would propel me towards shallower water.

After paddling underneath the jetty to the eastern side, I stared up at the jumping platform, but found no sign of life. The wind had eased, allowing me to rest, as gulls flew past, screeching in the half-light. Far ahead, I could see the welcoming lights of The Goose, a beachside restaurant that is popular with tourists and locals alike. I could even hear music and laughter drifting across the bay. While I bobbed on the water, diners would be enjoying drinks or studying menus, contemplating which share plate, house special or pizza to try.

During my last minutes on the water, I paddled slowly towards shore, thinking back to the trip to Donegal, six months earlier. If Charlie was alongside me now, he'd understand a little more about why I'd moved to Australia. It was close to dark when the kayak scraped its hull along the deserted beach. I dragged it away from the water, dropped my paddle and lay on the ground. In the silence that followed, I gazed into space and thought about my next adventure. Once again, I felt excited about living in Australia.

Wipeout

"Waves are not measured in feet and inches, they are measured in increments of fear."

– Buzzy Trent

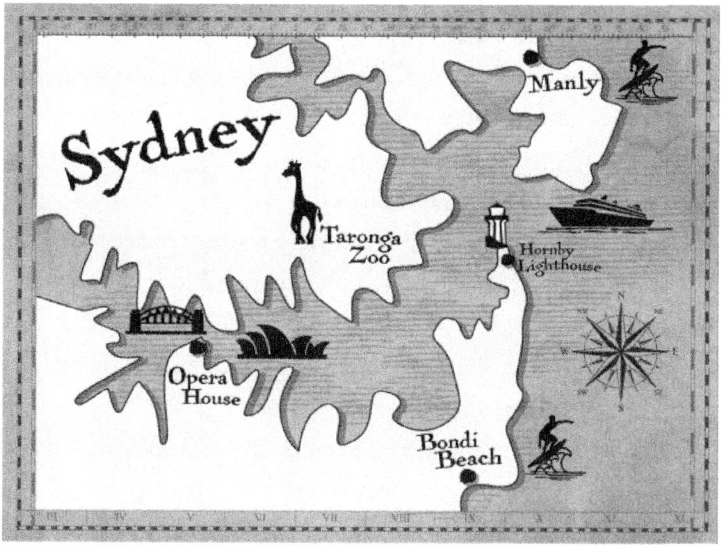

For many travellers to Australia, the east coast has the greatest appeal, with an abundance of summer sunshine and golden beaches that seem to stretch forever. Add surf spots to the mix, along with city nightlife, theme parks, national parks, coral reefs, coastal roads and hippy towns and you soon discover why many visitors run out of time to go anywhere else.

One of the most popular locations is Byron Bay, renowned for its laid-back vibe and tempting surf spots. Fran had travelled there while in her twenties and wanted to return, as part of her fiftieth birthday celebrations. Even though it had been nearly 30 years, she still talked about the crescent-shaped bay, fringed by a subtropical rainforest. During the family holiday, she also wanted to explore Sydney again, including the coastal suburb of Manly where she'd once lived and worked.

To get us from Perth to Sydney, I booked four economy seats on a Qantas flight. To travel 780 kilometres between Sydney and Byron Bay, we opted for something more adventurous. We were going to go on our first east coast, campervan road trip! A week before our departure, partway through the evening meal, I asked what we were all looking forward to during the holiday. Noah shrugged his shoulders and said, 'Dad, I'm not sure. I guess surfing would be fun, plus the zoo and a chance to go shopping.'

Sebastian went next and reeled off his wish-list, which included watching films on the flight, eating pizza in our hotel, bungee jumping, helicopter flights and surf lessons. I didn't have the heart to tell him we weren't booked into a hotel and as for the helicopter flight, that was way over budget! When it came to Fran's turn, she raised her wineglass and said, 'I want to go back and show you all the places I fell in love with. It's been far too long!'

Then she turned her attention towards the two boys, who were hoping by now to escape into the chill-out room for a quick play on their computer game before bedtime. 'Boys, did I tell you about the time I worked in and around

Sydney as a nanny for a company called Dial an Angel? I was in my early twenties and loved every minute of my time in Australia. Back then, I was footloose and fancy free.'

In response, Noah nodded, and Seby followed suit. After a brief pause, she continued without further prompts. 'Out of all the places on the east coast, I loved Sydney and Byron Bay the most. I loved the vibe, the sunshine, and the people I met along the way. I've been reading the guidebook and have made a list. First, I'd really like us to go cycling in Sydney, especially across the harbour bridge. Plus, we need to visit Taronga Zoo, the Royal Botanic Garden and China Town. If it's still there, I'd love to go inside the hostel in Glebe where I stayed before.'

While she took a trip down memory lane, we sat nearby, smiling at the stories as she rolled off a long list of must-see places. Somehow, it felt cruel to remind her we only had five days in Sydney, so I let her continue. When at last she stopped for breath, the boys scampered away. She didn't seem to notice, and after another sip of wine, she closed her eyes and continued.

She mentioned Manly, along with Bondi Beach, Sydney Opera House, Circular Quay, and a visit to the markets at Paddington. During the road trip, she also wanted to explore some of the coastal towns. As for our time in Byron Bay, she mentioned another bike ride, yoga on the beach, the chance to shop and an opportunity for the boys to surf the famous breaks.

A week later, during the flight from Perth to Sydney, I studied the guidebook a final time, trying not to be overwhelmed by the number of excursions, activities and attractions on offer. While Fran and the boys watched movies, I stared out of the window at the brown, featureless land, ten kilometres below, wondering how we'd fit everything in.

The interstate trip also gave us the perfect opportunity to try out Uber and Airbnb, the two powerhouses that are changing the way digital technology is being used in the travel industry. After touching down in Sydney, we followed the arrows towards baggage collection and then stepped into bright sunshine. As I'd hoped, the process of ordering a lift was seamless and within minutes we arrived at a designated pickup point for rideshare passengers. Soon, we were all enjoying complimentary bottles of cold water, dished out by our talkative driver who was keen to tell us about the lack of rain in recent weeks and the wilting heatwave refusing to budge.

For our stay in Sydney, we'd scoured the internet for an Airbnb close to Darling Harbour. During the drive, Fran peered out of the windows, searching for familiar landmarks, her eyes wide as she watched the city pass by. The apartment owner was standing outside his address as we pulled up. He helped with our luggage while pointing to the bright sky. 'It looks like you've brought the weather with you from Perth.'

During a leisurely tour of his stylish third-floor apartment, he showed us around each spotless room, before taking the time to explain the technicalities of using the dishwasher, smart TV and coffee maker. The tour finished with a visit onto his balcony to view the neighbouring apartments. Some balconies were hidden behind a swathe of clothes on washing lines. Other verandas had tropical plants housed in terracotta pots or portable barbeques and picnic chairs. One balcony was home to a ginger cat, lying across a railing three storeys from the ground!

The sight of a woman pegging washing across her veranda prompted the owner to lower his voice as he ushered us inside. 'They don't know I rent this place out, so if you meet anyone in the lift and they ask questions, just tell them you're my friends. I used to live here, but I've moved in with my partner and we now rent it out to help pay the mortgage. House prices and rentals are just crazy these days.'

He then left his name, contact details, a large bar of chocolate and a bottle of wine on the kitchen table, and gave the boys a high five. Just before leaving, he gave a few suggestions to get us through the heatwave. 'Drink plenty of water and get up early to enjoy the cooler weather.'

On our first evening, we set out to explore Darling Harbour and passed by a series of five-star hotels, some over 20 storeys high, before reaching a wooden boardwalk. As expected, the wharf had drawn a crowd, with a range of cafes, restaurants and bars to suit every taste and budget.

Despite the mouth-watering choices on offer, we opted for simplicity, enjoying fish and chips while gazing over the still waters towards the neon skyline. On such a balmy evening, with the smell of grilled fish competing with the waft of spices from a Chinese restaurant, it felt a world away from the place that would have once been a bustling port, filled with cranes, workmen and cargo ships. The animated banter between sailors and dockside workers is also a thing of the past, replaced by softly spoken words and gentle laughter from those enjoying their meals.

Initially known as Long Cove, the name was changed in 1826 by the governor, Ralph Darling. A lot has changed since then and the coastal steamers that supplied wool, wheat and coal to the wharves have been confined to the history books. The gradual demise of the working harbour began after the Second World War. The ship-building industry was in decline and container vessels had grown larger, which meant they could not dock alongside the finger wharves. Instead, they used the new, purpose-built terminal at Port Botany.

In 1984, the very last goods train set off from the yards, signalling the end of Darling Harbour as an industrious hub. During the same year, the Premier of New South Wales, Neville Wran, announced that the area would be redeveloped and returned to the people of Sydney.

In 1988, after extensive restorations, HM Queen Elizabeth II opened it to the public. Since then, it continues to attract millions of interstate and overseas visitors a year. Some come to experience the Sea Life Sydney Aquarium, one of the largest of its kind and home to over 700 different species of marine life. Others check out the maritime museum or the retail stores, before finishing their day with a waterfront dining experience.

After our fish and chips, the boys asked for a ride on the 35-metre-high Ferris wheel, situated close to the water's edge. As we sat in one of the enclosed pods, I gazed at the people walking below and those seated in the nearby restaurants. As our pod reached the top, I thought back to Neville Wran and his speech about the harbour being returned to the people of Sydney. From my bird's-eye view, I could see hundreds of people but had no idea how many of them were from Sydney. My guess was that they were just like us, relishing family time together while on holiday.

Although I enjoyed our evening in Darling Harbour, I couldn't help thinking we'd picked a location with a bright veneer, but little soul. With more time, I'd have stayed longer, to discover what made the place tick.

The following morning, we decided to hire bicycles and took a bus towards The Rocks, an elevated district, close to the southern side of the harbour. This historical suburb is regarded as the first permanent settlement of Europeans in Australia and was once used as a penal colony. The unusual name is derived from the sandstone blocks, used to construct many of the first buildings.

Much of the labour came from transported convicts, who lived in makeshift huts constructed from wattle and daub. Gamblers, prostitutes and vagabonds also made The Rocks their home, often living in rat-infested hovels, fabricated along the warren of nameless streets. The Rocks also attracted merchants, traders and the aristocratic, many of whom could afford to build grand houses, offering expansive views of the harbour.

Bubonic plague swept through many parts of Sydney in the 1900s, including The Rocks. To curb the disease, the city fathers decreed an order to demolish many of the cramped houses and shacks. Thankfully, the area didn't lose all its history to redevelopment and within minutes of stepping off the bus we found ourselves outside the Fortune of War, Sydney's oldest pub. Built in 1828 by the former convict Samuel Terry, the pub remains an integral part of the community.

For Samuel, Australia lived up to its reputation as being a *Lucky Country*.

He'd arrived in Australia as a chained convict with a sentence of seven years for the theft of 400 stockings. After being released, he turned his fortunes around and became a successful merchant, landowner and innkeeper.

Being so close to the wharf, the pub is often the first call for sailors and troops. In times of overseas conflict or international incidents, before setting sail, they congregate at the pub, where they also make plans to meet again on their return. The pub sits alongside a row of sandstone buildings. One of these was once a police station, but looked deserted as I peeked through the darkened windows. The other building looked far more inviting, revealing a cosy coffee shop on the site of a former bank.

Two large potted trees stood outside the pub's narrow frontage, with one in use as a resting place for a locked bicycle. I stopped for a moment to touch the shiny green tiles on the outside wall and to study a poster for an upcoming gig by a local musician. The doors and windows were wide open, offering the chance to catch sight of the late-morning patrons. There were no rowdy sailors or troops within view, just a handful of regulars, some reading newspapers and others propping up the bar, drinks in hand, chatting together.

In the heart of The Rocks, we strolled alongside welcoming cafés, each with their own outdoor setting. Sydney Harbour Bridge was rarely from sight, with each gap in the buildings revealing a section of its steel arches. With its hidden back streets, sandstone buildings, shaded walkways, funky cafés and boutique shops, I could already appreciate why the historical suburb holds such an appeal for visitors and locals alike. We found the bike hire shop a few minutes later, located partway along a cobbled alleyway, and stepped inside a narrow room filled with an assortment of bikes.

Although a polished steel fan whirred from behind the counter, for all its height and noise, it did little to stir the sultry air. While we flicked through promotional flyers, a wide-shouldered man of about 30 appeared from a back room. Wearing a flat cap and sporting a waxed moustache, he could well have been an extra from the TV show *Peaky Blinders*.

Any resemblance to early twentieth-century English Brummie soon vanished as he studied the boy's flushed faces and welcomed us in a familiar Aussie twang. 'You two lads look a bit frazzled. Why don't you head into the backyard and try out the water fountain? Say hello to Charlie while you're there. He loves a pat and won't bite, I promise.'

Without a backward glance, Noah and Sebastian ran off to investigate, prompting me to hold up one of the pamphlets. 'How's business today? It looks quiet around here. I guess most people are sunbathing instead of cycling.'

The owner smiled brightly and said, 'Far from it, mate. I've got one escorted tour out there now and another planned for this afternoon. Are you looking to join a tour or do your own thing?'

Fran took the lead and explained our plan. 'We'd like to hire some bikes for a few hours and are looking to explore the city.'

'No worries, but it'll be hot out there. Just go steady and take plenty of water. You can always book for this afternoon when it's due to be cooler.'

It was Fran who had the last word. 'No, this morning will be fine, thanks. My husband loves map reading and we can share the water between us.'

While Fran and the boys tried on their helmets, I paid the owner and signed some paperwork. He then helped with the adjustment of seats while I studied the complimentary map and tourist pamphlet, to find a few key facts that might impress them on the way. A quick scan revealed that when first opened, the cost to cross over Sydney Harbour Bridge by horse and cart was three pence. Since then, a lot has changed.

English currency has been replaced by the Australian dollar, and horses are no longer allowed to cross the bridge, unless being driven over in a box trailer. After many upgrades and engineering changes, the bridge now has seven vehicle lanes, a 24-hour bus lane, a designated cycle path, a walkway and two train lines!

We waved goodbye to the owner, freewheeled down the alleyway, crossed a one-way street and caught sight of a cruise ship, its glossy paintwork gleaming bright in the sunshine. An orderly queue of passengers stood on the quayside, protected from the drop into the water by a safety fence. The ship they were waiting to board was the largest I'd ever seen, and for a few minutes we stopped alongside to stare up at the many decks, each with row upon row of identical portholes. Apart from two sailors, dressed in white and standing alongside the wharf, there were no other crew members in sight.

Fran urged us away from the ship, towards a lookout point across the harbour, her voice raised to grab our attention. 'There it is. Look, there's Sydney Opera House. Boys, can you see it? Ali, have you got your camera?'

Then she pointed to her left. 'I'd forgotten how close the bridge is as well. Oh, how amazing!'

After a stop for photos, water, more photos and a toilet break, we coaxed Fran from the viewpoint and followed the map towards the base of the bridge. Known affectionately by the locals as the 'Coathanger' because of its arch-based design, the bridge loomed closer with every revolution of the pedals.

A set of steps then led us towards the designated bike path and we arrived at the top, panting and silent. After a stop for water, the boys sped ahead, prompting Fran to call them back, but the noise from passing traffic snatched away her words. Instead, she rode alongside me, chatting away while trying to absorb the sights and sounds. With the wind in our faces, we dropped through the gears and rode across the wide expanse of water towards the affluent suburb of Kirribilli.

We stopped once, to study the waterway and to stare into the mouth of the giant animated face that forms the entrance to Luna Park, the harbourside amusement park that's been on the same site since 1935. Since then, it has been through its own roller coaster ride with many stops and starts along the way, including a ghost train fire in 1979 that ended in the tragic death of seven people.

The ups and downs continued for many years after, despite extensive developments taking place. Thankfully, since 2004, it has remained open, and because of its waterfront location, Art déco styling and choice of modern and traditional rides, is still a major attraction for locals and visitors alike.

The boys were waiting on the far side, and together we carried the bikes down a wide set of steps and under the bridge. We'd been cycling for about 30 minutes and according to the map, had ridden about ten percent of our planned route. Seby pointed to a nearby delicatessen and asked, 'Dad, can I have an ice cream, please? I'm boiling!'

His freckled cheeks were flushed and the trademark smile was in danger of turning into a weary scowl. I wanted to say yes, but our journey had only just started. Once inside the delicatessen, we might never leave. I pushed away the feeling of guilt and said, 'Have some water first, then I'll race you back across the bridge to find somewhere nice that serves ice cream and cold drinks.'

In response, he turned towards his mum. 'That's not fair. Can I have an ice cream or lemonade? I'm so hot! Please!'

'Come on,' she said, 'I'll race you to the top.'

Without waiting for a reply, Fran picked up her bike and climbed the steps that would lead us back onto the bridge. We were now on the eastern side of the bridge, on a pathway designated for pedestrians. With no one in sight, we saddled up and made our way towards the city.

With the wind at our backs, the return leg was easier, allowing us to ride in close formation. To our right, a steady stream of traffic drove past, segregated by crash barriers. In a moment of silence, I pulled the pamphlet from my pocket and called out for attention. 'Listen up, everyone. Whoever guesses the nearest number wins a double-choc ice cream.

How many hand-driven rivets are used to hold the bridge together?'

'What's a hand-driven rivet?' Noah asked, as he made a move to overtake me.

I pointed to the steel ramparts and said, 'Look around you–the rivets are everywhere. They're like giant-sized pop rivets, made from steel.'

'A thousand,' Seby yelled from up front.

'A million,' Noah replied.

'Look, there's Sydney Opera House,' Fran called out.

She then stopped by the side of the track and waved us down. 'Ali, have you got your camera? The harbour looks amazing. Can you get us all in for a picture?'

'Six million,' I said.

'Six million what?' she asked.

'Rivets. Just rivets.'

I pulled out my camera as they stood arm in arm. 'Seby, look at me. Perfect. Now altogether, say, happy faces!'

No amount of photos from an amateur photographer like myself can capture the feeling of what it's like to stand on one of the most famous bridges in the world. Far in the distance, a glint of sunshine on the white-sailed roof of Sydney Opera House held my attention.

I also spotted boats and ships of every size and description, making their way across the bay. Some, like the cruise ship docked at Circular Quay, looked capable of carrying thousands of passengers to the other side of the world. Others, like the Sydney ferries, their familiar racing-green and cream colours a part and parcel of the landscape, carry over 14 million passengers between them each year. Fran pointed to a sailing boat far below us, and we watched it change tack before heading under the bridge, its sails twitching in the breeze as a lone seagull glided above the milky wake.

We could have stayed on the bridge all morning, to study the coves and inlets and gaze at the city skyline, but with water supplies dwindling, refreshments were high on the agenda. While we prepared to leave, Fran took hold of my hand and steered me towards the mesh barrier that protected us from the long drop to the water. 'Ali, do you realise this city was once my home? Not for long, but enough to make a lasting impression. In all that time, I never crossed over the bridge like this. Somewhere out there, amongst the beachside suburbs, is Manly, where I once lived. Can you believe it's taken me so long to return?'

It was Seby that broke the spell, calling out for us to get a move on and asking how long before we could stop for an ice cream. As we approached the far side, we stopped once more, to watch the ant-like figures far above, climbing the steel ramparts to stand on the very top of the bridge. We'd return to the bridge another day and exchange bikes for climbing harnesses, but for now, all thoughts were on ice creams and cold drinks.

On our return to the heart of the city, we came across a four-storey building, on a street corner within The Rocks precinct. Noah noticed a swinging sign above the doorway, declaring that we were about to enter the Lord Nelson, the oldest continually licensed hotel in Sydney. Originally built as a two-storey residence, using sandstone blocks quarried by convicts, the owner, William Wells, obtained a liquor license in 1841. The establishment was named after his naval hero and has remained open until this day.

The sun was high, casting few shadows, although those seated outside were able to shelter under wide canopies while enjoying drinks in the heat of the day. The interior was cooler, helped by ceiling fans and open windows. After we'd parked ourselves around a long wooden table, we picked our way through a leisurely lunch, followed by ice cream desserts. Throughout the meal, Fran continually raided the communal fridge for complimentary water and topped up our glasses. I didn't want to leave without sampling one of the craft beers brewed on the premises and stood by the bar, admiring the names of each one written on a chalkboard.

While the barman poured a pint of *Three Sheets*, I wandered towards a set of framed photos adorning a brick wall, depicting naval figureheads from long ago, including a striking image of Lord Nelson in uniform. With beer in hand, I studied many of the other framed photos and memorabilia on display and soon began thinking about my dad. He'd once been a merchant seaman and had travelled to Sydney in his early twenties, after setting sail from Greenock, Scotland. He'd been the type of character who would have enjoyed The Rocks of old, with its lively taverns, simple lodgings and charismatic locals.

Maybe he'd stood at the bar in the Lord Nelson during a night on the town with his crewmates. There was no way of knowing anymore, but I smiled at the thought while enjoying my drink. As we left the hotel bar, I made a show of folding the map into two before storing it in my daypack. Seby was watching, and before he made a comment, I said, 'I don't know about you three, but I'm just about ready for a swim.'

All heads turned towards Fran, who nodded in agreement. 'An afternoon at the beach sounds perfect,' she said. 'Mind you, I've really enjoyed the bike ride. I just wish we'd started earlier in the day.'

We rode downhill towards the bike shop, and returned the bikes to their owner, who received them with a wry smile. We then took a short stroll to Circular Quay, stopping on the way to listen to an Aboriginal playing the didgeridoo. He was dressed in traditional attire, with tiny white dots painted across his youthful face and lean body. He'd drawn a large crowd and played the instrument with pride. The hypnotic sound followed us along the dockside, as we threaded our way through the crowd towards the ferry terminals.

Fran studied the timetables on each wharf and stopped alongside the end one. 'This is where we need to catch our ferry. It's all coming back to me now. While working as a nanny, I stayed in Manly for a few weeks with a lovely family. I used to take the children on the ferries most days.'

Before she had time to dwell any further, the wharf came to life with the arrival of a ferry. It docked alongside, allowing one set of passengers to get off and another to get on. Throughout the hustle and bustle of passengers in transit, I watched the deckhands as they steadied the ferry, expertly coiling ropes around securing points and setting up a ramp between the ferry and quayside.

The captain gave a toot of the horn to signal our departure and with a rev of the engines and the churning of water we were on our way. After leaving the quayside, we were soon rewarded with up-close and personal views of the white-sailed roof of Sydney Opera House, standing proud against a cloudless sky. The ferry then turned towards the suburb of Manly, on the far side of the water.

While Fran took photos, I climbed to the upper deck with the boys, and together we stared out across the dark water, towards Sydney Harbour Bridge as it straddled the harbour. Despite the impressive views on offer, some passengers remained seated and rarely looked up from their books, magazines or smartphones. Maybe they were Sydneysiders who had grown used to the daily commute alongside some of the most iconic landmarks in Australia.

The scene reminded me of a time a year earlier. During a trip to London, we'd visited Camden Market one Sunday to browse amongst the hundreds of stalls selling everything from vintage fashion to handcrafted gifts. While Fran and the boys stopped to sample Korean street food, I stole away to take photos of the alleyways and brick-built arches, then sat for a while to admire colourful narrow boats chugging along Regent's Canal. To those who live and work in London, there was nothing new to see. But I'd visited from Australia and couldn't get enough of the sights, sounds and smells of the famous market. While I snapped away, trying to capture the moment, the locals walked past, eyes straight, accustomed to their historical surroundings.

We soon learned that visitors to Manly are spoilt for choice, with the option of lazing on the family-friendly beach next to the ferry terminal or taking a stroll towards the other side of the peninsula, which faces the Pacific Ocean. Within the space of three hours, we tried both. The calm bay next to the quayside proved a popular location for families. While toddlers played in the shallows, teenagers strutted along the wharf, before jumping into the deeper water.

After we'd settled on the beach, I held up my GoPro camera and laid down a challenge to Noah. 'If you jump off the jetty, I'll tread water nearby to get a photo of you in mid-air.'

'Sure, Dad. I'll be there in a minute.'

With a bounce in his stride, he scampered towards the jetty steps while I set off towards deeper water. Initially, I stayed in the shallows, alongside the wooden pylons that support the wharf. With each step away from the beach, I noticed shoals of tiny fish, flashing past in the sea green water. I held the GoPro underwater, eager to get a close-up of the fish, and stepped forward. In an instant, my right foot exploded with pain and I let out a cry, before falling backwards and clutching my leg. My initial thought was that an electrical current had zapped me.

At that moment, a teenage girl was close by, having leapt from the wharf a few seconds earlier. She swam past, her shrill words impossible to miss. 'Watch out! That man's been bitten.'

From the wharf someone shouted 'shark' and within seconds those around me were swimming frantically towards the beach. By now I was swimming on my back towards the shallows, fighting the urge to scream as a lightning bolt tore through the sole of my foot. After reaching the water's edge, I lay my head on the sand, oblivious to the surrounding crowd. Fran rushed to my side and as I chewed on my lip and closed my eyes, she peered and prodded the sole of my foot. I then heard a deep voice, calling out, 'Stand aside, stand aside!'

As I opened my eyes, the sun was blocked by the sight of a grey-haired man dressed in bathing shorts, with prominent ribs and a dark tan. Without prompting, he said, 'It could have been an urchin, but if there's no barb, I'd say you stood on a numb ray. They deliver a nasty shock, so it's no wonder you look pasty. They're not that common, so you were lucky to discover one. You'll be fine in a while. Just wait and see.'

And then he was gone and Noah was by my side, asking when I'd be okay to take the mid-air photo! With no blood, gore or torn limbs to report, the onlookers silently dispersed, and within seconds the water was filled with swimmers again.

The main beach is situated a short walk from the quayside, through a pedestrianised strip known as Manly Corso, tastefully adorned with rows of palm trees. On either side of the walkway were a multitude of bistros, bars and trendy surf stores. While I recovered on a bench, Fran and the boys went in search of takeaway ice creams. By the time we'd finished them, the throb in my foot began to ease.

A leisurely stroll led us towards another pedestrianised area. This one ran parallel with the wide beach and offered walkers, runners and cyclists the chance to enjoy the ocean view while cruising past. All eyes were on the Pacific Ocean, but unlike the quayside bay, this stretch of water looked far livelier. Most of the shoreline was being pounded by rollers, and despite the heat, there were few people in the water. The lifeguards had planted red flags along the beach at regular intervals, as a warning to swimmers to stay out of the water. To ensure the message hit home, there were other signs, displaying the international symbol for 'No Swimming.'

As we kicked off our shoes and stepped onto the beach, I spotted a notice board, displaying the forecast temperature, wind conditions and wave size. I had no idea if a two-metre swell was a good thing, but 32 degrees on the thermometer told me we deserved a dip in the water. We'd have to choose the right spot though, as bold words written across the notice board warned of rip currents close by.

Rip currents are one of the most dangerous natural hazards in the aquatic world, causing multiple deaths each year, and are part of the reason why surf-lifesaving clubs are so important. The rip is often a narrow but powerful current, which runs away from the beach, towards open water. Those caught in a rip can quickly lose their strength if they try swimming against it. The safest option is to swim between the red-and-yellow flags, where the lifeguards patrol.

Further to our right the ocean was filled with dozens of swimmers, staying within sight of two red-and-yellow flags, fluttering in the breeze. Fran and the boys set off, eager for a dip, and I promised to catch up to them. But first I wanted to watch the lifeguards, who were easily recognisable by their bright tops and red-and-yellow bathing caps. There were a handful on duty, including one girl patrolling the beach on a quad bike. She looked to be about eighteen and handled the machine with confidence while driving across the rutted sand. Others manned a portable beach shelter, their eyes focused on the water.

As I approached the last red flag before the designated swimming area, I stopped alongside a lifeguard. She was about 20 years of age, her eyes hidden behind wraparound sunglasses, with blonde hair struggling to stay contained under her bathing cap. Her mouth held a whistle that she blew in a series of loud blasts, to gain the attention of a potbellied man dressed in bathers, knee-deep in water while heading towards distant waves.

Within a few steps he was waist-deep, triggering the lifeguard into action as she raced towards the shallows, her whistle piercing the air. Finally, he stopped and looked around, as if checking what all the noise was for. As he was the only person in this part of the ocean, it made sense that he was the centre of her attention. She removed the whistle and called out, 'Yes mate, I'm looking at you. There's a strong current and you need to get out of the water. Haven't you seen the signs?'

Then she pointed to the dozens of swimmers and surfers in front of the red-and-yellow flags and instructed him to join them. He stepped towards the beach, floundering as a wave pounded his lower back, then found his footing and strode onto the damp sand. Without a word, he reached for the sunglasses secured through a mass of greying curls, put them on and strutted along the beach towards the red-and-yellow flags. With no other apparent distractions, I stepped nearer and called out above the sound of the crashing waves. 'I guess you're having a busy day.'

She gave me a sideways glance and managed a half smile. 'No, mate, it's just a typical day, with the usual amount of people that think they're invincible. Now, how can I help you?'

I was momentarily lost for words, so just grinned and said, 'No, I'm fine and was just passing the time. I'll get back to my wife and kids.'

She seemed to relax a little and said, 'Watch out for the bluebottles, mate. We found a few this morning and if the wind picks up, they may blow our way, which means we'll probably close the beach.'

I'd heard about the blue, balloon-like jellyfish, with long tentacles that inject painful toxins, but wasn't aware they were prevalent in the area. She seemed eager to share her knowledge and said, 'Mate, if there are blueys on the beach, stay away from the water. They may look small and pretty, but they can rip your skin to shreds.'

'What do you do if you get stung?' I asked.

'Use seawater to rinse the area and then clean the sting in hot water. Forget the vinegar, though. Keep that for your fish and chips. Now if you'll excuse me, I need to talk to one of my teammates.'

With that, she strolled towards the lifeguard shelter while I turned my attention to the ocean, watching surfers glide along the face of two-metre waves, far from Fran and the boys, who were swimming in calmer waters. Our trip to Manly ended with a fish and chip supper, in one of the many seafront cafes. I asked for the catch of the day and got served a battered fillet of flathead, along with a bowl of delectable chips. While we tucked in, gulls swept overhead or paraded along the pavement, searching for scraps as locals and tourists sat side by side, enjoying the warm evening air and the sound of rollers crashing onto an empty beach.

During our time in the city, we discovered that the giraffes in Taronga Zoo have an enviable view of the skyscrapers from their leafy enclosure. We also learned that the Sydney Opera House has six different venues underneath its sails. With up to 40 shows on offer each week, the ever-changing choices are wide ranging. From opera to punk and everything in between, including world-renowned dancers, comedians and actors.

To help get around, we purchased Opal smart cards, which gave us the opportunity to travel by bus, rail or boat. After studying a map, we boarded a bus to Paddington Markets for the chance to shop for locally produced gifts. There was something for everyone, including stalls offering homemade crafts and an outdoor setting filled with food vans selling tasty delights. One stallholder we all enjoyed was owned by a family of Chinese healers, offering the chance of a therapeutic massage while lazing under the welcoming shade of gum trees.

The suburb of Bondi is where you will find one of Australia's most famous beaches. Its sweeping bay is home to lucrative apartments, with some residents lucky enough to enjoy panoramic views of the waves that tempt surfers from across the world. The curved, golden beach, vibrant social scene and laid-back atmosphere add to its appeal and it was here that Fran enjoyed breakfast on her fiftieth birthday.

She picked a café with an ocean view and we sat alongside locals and tourists, all enjoying the early morning sunshine. While waiting for our food to arrive, Fran opened her birthday cards. As she read each one out loud, surfers passed by, their boards held tightly as they skateboarded towards the beach.

An hour later, we joined them on the beach and soon discovered that surf lessons were in high demand. Instead, we hired body boards, then weaved our way through the crowds and searched for a vacant patch of sand. Before we entered the ocean, the boys searched for silted water close to shore and explained about rip currents. I smiled in acknowledgment that the recent surf lessons they'd taken back home were now paying off.

As expected, the boys sought out the largest of the swells, leaving their parents to tackle the tamer waves. Fran took to it with ease, gliding along the crest of each roller and calling out for me to venture deeper. I body surfed a few waves, before spinning upside down and getting caught in the wash. I tried again, getting braver by the minute, until caught off guard. The force of the wave pushed me under, spun me around and spat me onto the beach in front of a passing lifeguard. She smiled as I dragged my board from the water's edge and mumbled something about needing a drink.

While searching for a water fountain, I stopped alongside the lifeguard station. A side door was open, offering the chance to spot lifeguards watching through the tinted windows, their eyes peeled for signs of distress or wayward swimmers. I'd seen the lookout hut many times, while watching the hit TV show *Bondi Rescue*. Since its inaugural broadcast in 2006, the show has become a worldwide hit.

With endless sunshine, warm sand, powerful waves and thousands of visitors eager to enjoy the experience, there is rarely a dull moment at Bondi during the summer. Throughout this period, the cameras capture the highs, lows and watery escapades, which have made some lifeguards into household names.

By the time I returned from my walk, Fran and the boys were drying themselves down and seemed eager to escape from the waves. After returning the boards, we investigated Bondi Baths, within walking distance at the southern edge of the bay. For a modest fee, we could use the plush facilities of the Bondi Icebergs Club, which included a swim in the lap pools.

Fran took the boys to search for the baths while I ordered a cold beer and searched for a vacant spot on the balcony. From my vantage point, the furthest bath resembled an infinity pool–such was its closeness to the ocean. As Seby sat on the side with his toes dipped in the water, a surfer paddled close by, just beyond the whitewashed walls.

While they swam multiple lengths to prepare for an event back home, I investigated the open-plan bar. Soon, I was standing by a freshly painted wall, admiring the various awards and merits that have been handed out over the years. I also discovered that to become a member of the Bondi Icebergs Club requires a concerted effort.

To qualify, you need to swim three out of four Sundays between the cooler months of May until September and need to achieve a minimum of 75 swims over five years. Juniors are also encouraged and are known as Icecubes, until they turn 18, when they are welcome to join the Icebergs!

Fran and the boys arrived at the bar soon after, eager for refreshments. While seated on the veranda, we tucked into fish and chips, listening to the shrill of whistles as Bondi lifeguards directed wayward swimmers away from danger.

After the meal, we studied our map and decided on a leisurely walk to the beachside suburb of Coogee. Every twist and turn on the footpath revealed a different view of the ocean, as it lapped against a series of rocky inlets and sandy coves. Along the way, we stopped for ice creams, took spontaneous dips in the ocean, spotted lizards basking on the rocks, and found the time to talk to dog walkers while patting their panting pets.

After a stop in Coogee for welcome drinks at a beachside pub, we headed back to the apartment by taxi for a shower and change. By sunset, we were enjoying dinner at an outdoor restaurant next to the Sydney Opera House, and within full view of the bridge. To the sound of a passing ferry tooting its horn, we clinked glasses, raised a birthday toast to Fran, and agreed to return another day.

In hindsight, we should have taken more time to relax during our time in the city. It is blessed with wide-open spaces, including the Royal Botanic Garden, a 74-acre site that wraps around the headland. But our time in Sydney was now over, and the following morning I called for a taxi.

During our drive to the campervan pickup location, I couldn't hold back the widest of grins. After so many years of living in Australia, we'd finally be on a road trip along the east coast. By Australian standards it would not be a long journey, but I didn't care. Sometime today we'd be cruising north along the freeway, with the sun overhead and the smell of sea salt in the air.

The rental company was housed in an industrial estate, with a wide selection of caravans and campervans on display outside. These, I figured, were recent returns, now serviced and washed for the next set of customers. I'd booked our van a month earlier, thinking there would still be an abundance of choices, despite the onset of summer. The stark reality that had faced me from the online booking form was that most options were sold out, apart from a vehicle described as 'cosy, but comfortable' and ideal for those on a budget. The only other option had been twice as large and double the price.

After stepping into the cool interior of the large, open-plan room, I gazed at the far wall to study a giant map of the east coast of Australia, depicting the cities, towns and natural attractions, all linked by a network of roads. The route we were about to embark on would only scratch the surface compared to all the other locations on offer. I smiled at the thought of undertaking a longer trip next time and turned my attention to the front desk.

A retired couple had just handed in a set of keys to a receptionist and were promising to return next year for another three-month trip. They ambled past, arm in arm, their smiling faces ripened by the sun.

At the front desk we handed over our details to a young, red-haired woman. She had a polite smile and fast fingers, which found our booking within a few keystrokes. 'Oh yes, here you are, Mr. and Mrs. McGuinness. It looks like you've booked a four-berth campervan for seven days, including Wi-Fi and a camping table.'

She peered over the counter at the family of four staring back, each person slightly smaller in height, finishing with

Seby's green eyes, watching with interest. While gazing at her computer screen, she said, 'So, if you're interested, there's a chance to go for a—'

'Dad, what are these for?'

Seby had wandered off and was now standing alongside a display of tinned and packaged goods, stored on a rack. The assistant overheard and said, 'That's the free-cycle section. It's a great system and you can take what you like. All we ask is that you return the favour when you drop the van off at Brisbane.'

Fran took the initiative and completed the booking while I investigated the giveaways with Seby. While we selected spices, cooking oil and a brand-new packet of silver foil, Fran appeared at my side, with the campervan keys jangling in her hand.

We were joined in the car park by the same assistant who then gave me a handover while Fran and the boys stowed the luggage. After sliding open the side door, she pointed to a small melamine table sandwiched between two foam seats. 'The table folds down with a twist of the handle and the bedding is under the seats. Power and water are connected at the back of the van, and as I'm sure you know, we drive on the left.'

While she pointed out each feature, my mind whirred with questions. I should have taken the time to ask them, but with the sun beating down on my exposed scalp, the thought of being on the open road proved too tempting. After finishing the polished spiel, she said, 'If you have any more questions, just pop inside before you go as there's a lot to take in. We're open until six, so you can always call.'

We shook hands and she returned to the reception area, just as Fran appeared by my side. 'Isn't this exciting? Do you know how it all works?'

I feigned confidence and said, 'Yes, we're good to go. It can't be that hard as it's just a budget campervan, after all.'

'But Ali, we don't have to—'

Just then, Noah called out from the rear seats. 'Mum, my seat belt is jammed. Can you help me, please?'

While she sorted out the boys, I started the engine, cranked the air conditioner, turned on the GPS and searched for Port Macquarie on the screen. A few minutes later, we were on the road, following the instructions from the mapping device while listening to the persistent beat of a hip-hop song from the radio. While Fran searched for another station, I slid on my sunglasses, wound down the window, and let my arm flop against the warm panelling, grinning widely in anticipation of what lay ahead.

After breaking free of the industrial estate, we were soon hurtling along a three-lane highway. Fran's eyes were glued to the GPS screen, which not only displayed a map but also emitted a robotic female voice, instructing me to take the next available turn. I was in the middle lane and the traffic to my left was tightly bunched, with hardly a gap between bumpers. Fran turned down the radio to grab my attention. 'Ali, the exits coming up. Are you watching the screen?'

The robotic voice agreed, telling me I had to take a left turn in 800 metres. The sight of brake lights, followed by daylight between two cars offered the gap I needed, and I raced ahead, intent on making the move. As I pulled into the left lane, a dual carriageway merged with the highway, filled with cars and trucks.

I now had two additional lanes to cross and while searching for another gap, the robotic voice instructed me to take the exit in 200 metres. Fran joined in with the commands while pointing to the exit sign. 'Just slow down and force your way through. They'll let you in. This is Sydney!'

Suddenly, the exit was upon us and we were being forced downstream, hemmed in on all sides by hundreds of vehicles. As the exit slipway dwindled from view, the robotic voice came to life with the words I dreaded to hear. *Turn around and proceed to the route.* In response, Fran threw her hands in the air and said, 'You just don't listen, do you!'

We drove in silence along the carriageway, searching for another suitable exit, but they'd all vanished. Soon after, we caught sight of the white-sailed roof of Sydney Opera House. At the same time, the robotic voice came back to life, offering us a way out of the city, and this time I was prepared to hustle.

The Pacific Highway runs parallel with the coastline for over 700 kilometres, starting north of Sydney, before merging with other major roads. During the drive, we travelled through a fertile landscape of woodland and farms, including two wide rivers, the Karuah and the Manning. We stopped a few times, either to admire boats on the water, or to stretch our legs in one of the country towns while in search of a snack. Most towns had a tavern, a bakery and a parade of shops, along with tourist accommodation ranging from caravan parks to hotels and motels.

Six hours later we were in a campsite, close to the coastal town of Port Macquarie. The sun was dropping slowly, taking its sting with it, but the humidity refused to budge. All around me I could see activity, as families prepared for barbeques and children played on nearby swings or splashed in the pool. The camp had numbered plots, spaced evenly throughout seven acres of manicured grounds. With peak season approaching, many spots were taken, but they'd allocated us a section with vacant lots to either side of our campervan.

While I set up camp, the boys made a bid for freedom and headed to nearby trees for the chance to explore. Fran was next to leave me, in search of the communal shower block. Suddenly alone, I cracked open a cold beer, relishing the late afternoon sunshine as I searched for a summer tune to play on our portable speaker.

As I pottered around camp, Fran arrived back on the scene, recommending I use the cold water to wash in. Beads of sweat had already formed on her brow during the short walk across the campsite, but at least she no longer smelt as bad as I did. I wore a sweat-stained singlet and grubby shorts, along with a pair of sandals that had seen better days. Not only did I need a shower, but a change of outfit.

The shower would come soon, but it had been a long day and the nearest restaurant was now cooking our takeaway. After pouring a wine for Fran, I held my beer up high in a toast. 'The setup looks great. I just need to put up the awning and we'll be ready for tomorrow's sunshine.'

She took a sip of her drink and leaned closer. 'I'm not sure if you're aware, but we don't have an awning. They offered us one this morning, but I think you got distracted by the giveaways.'

I dismissed her comments as a joke and made a move towards the van to locate the missing awning. She followed closely and said, 'I'm sorry, Ali, but there's no point looking, as we haven't got one.'

Before I could reply, she followed up with a counter-punch. 'We were also offered an upgrade while you were searching for free curry powder. I should have said, but you seemed happy with the van as it is.'

'Upgrade? What do you mean?'

'It would have cost more, but the receptionist said she had a van with bigger beds, air-con, a TV and an awning.'

'Fran, right now we're close to the border with Queensland, which isn't known as the sunshine state for nothing. It's one of the hottest places, in one of the hottest countries in the world! In such a place, air conditioning and awnings need to be a standard feature.'

'Maybe it won't be too hot this evening,' she suggested, as a trickle of sweat ran down her neck. I shook my head in disbelief, trying to fathom how we'd missed out on the opportunity to upgrade. I then had a sudden thought and asked her for the time.

'It's nearly six o'clock,' she said. 'That reminds me, our takeaway will be ready.'

'Just a second. I need to make a call.'

I recognised the assistant on the other end of the phone and quickly explained our plight while listening to her fingers tap on the keyboard. After a pause, she gave her answer. 'I wondered why you didn't opt for an upgrade.'

'But why didn't you say?'

'I explained to your wife, and to be truthful, during the handover you looked happy enough.'

'I was happy. The happiest in years! But I'm feeling foolish now about missing out on some shade. Is there a place I can hire one from?'

'I wouldn't think so. If you try to fit one and cause a problem, you won't be covered on the insurance.'

'What do we do about sitting outside the van? Without an awning, we'll just fry.'

'I'm sorry, sir. I see from the booking that your campsite at Port Macquarie has a pool and a few shady spots, which you could have secured, if you'd booked earlier. At least you can put it down to experience.'

Before the call ended, I had one last question to ask. 'In all the times you've worked each summer, has anyone ever said no to an awning or the chance of air conditioning?'

There was a slight pause, followed by the sound of finger tapping. Then she said, 'Funny you say that, as I think you were the first family ever.'

After the call ended, I grabbed a water bottle before ambling up a nearby embankment to sit beside a row of pine trees. Fran joined me soon after, noting we now had an ocean view and reminding me once more that I used to have a sense of adventure!

She was right, of course. It was only an awning, but I should have checked before insisting on a hasty departure. My impatience had cost us a little luxury. Every other tent, campervan, camper trailer and caravan that we could see from our vantage point had awnings of some type. Some were elongated strips of fabric, secured from rooflines and angled to deflect the rain or shield the sun. Others resembled Bedouin tents, their guy ropes stretched to the edges of each plot.

Fran seemed eager to look for the positives and gave a wide smile. 'Let's put it down to experience, and at least it isn't raining. Besides, we're off to Byron Bay in a few days and I'll phone ahead to see if we can secure a shady spot.'

While she spoke, I heard rubber on gravel and glanced towards the camp entrance, its boom gate opening to allow a vehicle to pass through. It was the type of oversized camper-van that I'd only ever seen in American road movies, where dysfunctional families, headed by the likes of Chevy Chase, cause mayhem and mischief as they blunder their way across the Rocky Mountains to escape city life.

As it drove past our camping spot, we studied its tinted windows and noted a satellite dish positioned alongside an air conditioning unit. I expected the van to keep going, towards the larger plots, closer to the ocean. Instead, it slowed to a halt, sending a cloud of red dirt into the air as the tyres bit into the gravel.

For a few seconds, all was quiet, until the moment the driver selected their reverse gear, which triggered a shrill beeper into life. We were about to meet our new neighbours. Being such an extravagant vehicle, it took some time to manoeuvre into position alongside our cosy van.

Finally, just like a jet airplane that has arrived at its destination after a long flight, the engine was shut down. A few moments later, the driver's door inched open. The man that stepped into the sunlight had a full head of jet-black hair, a slow swagger and a sun-kissed face. He looked to be in his early forties, dressed in a sea-blue Polo shirt, matching shorts and leather sandals. I waved a greeting and got a nod in reply as he wandered to the back of his vehicle, pulled out two electrical leads and plugged them into the allocated sockets on a nearby post. He then switched on the power, before turning his attention to a lock-up box filled with tools.

The second person to emerge from the cab looked younger, thinner and taller, with designer sunglasses, an all-over tan and short blonde hair. She wore the type of flowing shawl glamorised in art movies and stood to one side to watch an awning automatically swing down from the rooftop.

As the man returned to the scene to hook up a water supply, it dawned on me that their palace on wheels was just for the two of them, although it could easily house a football team. There were no children running amok, no crazy pets to add to the mix, or toddlers playing. In contrast, our budget campervan, just yards away, would have fitted into their master bedroom.

They were now standing within view–him adjusting a dial–her checking a phone screen. Then he called out, 'Try that, Deidre. The shower should work now. I'll turn the air conditioning on and then we can wander into town for a sundowner.'

Hours later, I was cocooned in our van, forced inside by mosquitoes that had feasted on my exposed ankles. Now, scratching, cursing and sweating, while sitting under the muted glow of the overhead lamps, I played Travel Monopoly with my family.

That's what I was supposed to be doing, but during Noah's roll of the dice I'd adjusted the curtains to gaze up at the van next door. Through a gap in their blinds, I could see the edge of a wide-screen TV, playing a Netflix show. Earlier, I'd returned from the toilet block to hear the whirr of their air conditioning unit and had stood alongside their van, admiring the grandeur of such luxury.

Fran had stepped outside to investigate my whereabouts and found me standing in the moonlight, bathed in sweat while staring up at the van. She handed me a bottle of water and said, 'Come back inside, Ali. You'll get bitten by the mozzies and we have a game of Monopoly to finish.'

As she ushered me home, I pointed to next door's van. 'Doesn't it look amazing. Do you think they have a battery backup system as well as everything else?'

Her voice dropped to a whisper. 'Why would you be asking about that? You're not thinking for one minute about disconnecting their power, are you? That's ridiculous and mean-spirited.'

'No, of course not. But wouldn't it be great to see them looking like boiled lobsters in the morning, just like we'll be!'

Our sleeping arrangements included a cramped double bed (once Seby had worked out how to unscrew the tabletop) and another bed upstairs. I say upstairs, but there were no steps, unless you counted the fact that you had to stand on the kitchenette counter, hoping your feet didn't slide into the sink.

Then you eased into the allocated space, made from wide pieces of plyboard wedged horizontally between rails, an arm's length from the roof. This narrow gap resembled the interior of a baker's van, and it was here that Noah and Seby were persuaded to spend their first ever night in a campervan, while lying side by side on a foam bed. If any fresh air made it their way, it came through the insect mesh, positioned behind the narrow side window, which had been opened wide. I lay five feet below them alongside Fran, both of us fidgety and sweaty in the close confines, yearning for the night to end.

The following morning, after a cold shower and a dip in the pool, I went on a shopping spree and returned with a portable fan and a multi-pack of icebox coolers, which were stored in the camp freezer until I'd prepared a strategy for nightfall. After a day on the beach, Fran and the boys prepared dinner, while I went running along the coastal footpath. I kept going until my legs turned to jelly, hoping that exhaustion and a six-pack of locally crafted beers would help me sleep through the night.

By sunset we were sitting peacefully outside our campervan, enjoying drinks while trying out the natural mosquito repellent that Fran had discovered at the local shops. There was only one more thing to do before bedtime, which meant a visit to the communal kitchen to collect the frozen icepacks.

On my return, I walked past our neighbours. They were sitting by a lantern, enjoying drinks and nibbles, while reading in the soft glow. I called out a greeting and gained a casual nod by the man, as he studied the frozen icepacks before returning to his book.

Walking back into our campervan felt like stepping into a sauna. With an eager smile, I pointed towards the new fan and called out for attention. I didn't need to raise my voice as each of us looked to be within arm's reach. 'Okay, so this is the main feature of our homemade air-conditioning unit. All we need to do is—'

Before I could explain, Fran cut me off mid-stride. 'Ali, it's just a portable fan with two speeds. My hairdryer has more gumption than that.'

I held up a hand, warding away any more negativity. 'It might look like a cheap fan, but this could make our night if it works properly.'

Seby bravely added his thoughts while pointing to the fan. 'Dad, all it will do is blow hot air around. We need a cool breeze and can't open the door because of the mozzies.'

I then revealed our secret weapon, by breaking open the multi-pack of colourful icepacks. 'Exactly, Seby. That's why we'll be using these!'

Within minutes we'd strung them across the interior of the van, with the largest blocks positioned as close to the whirring blades as I dared. The remainder were placed under our thin blankets, to help cool the beds. Once complete, we drew cards to see who had to clamber to the upper bed, via the kitchenette counter. Thankfully for me, the boys drew the wrong cards and set off on their brief journey, armed with torches, water and the rest of the frozen icepacks.

Just as before, I lay five feet below them, side by side with Fran. In the darkness, I heard the whirring of the fan, competing with the drone of a persistent mosquito. In the moments before sleep, I lifted a hand into the air, feeling thankful for the cool breeze wafting overhead.

By midnight, I was wide-awake, bathed in sweat and suffering from a crooked neck. My bladder was bursting from the six-pack of beers and the toilet block was 100 metres away. I reached out and touched the nearest icepack. As feared, it was as warm as toast.

I made my way outside, and then dashed for the nearest tree, thankful for the moonlight that bathed the camp in a soft glow. I stopped to listen for the ocean and for a few moments, enjoyed the sound of distant waves rolling onto the beach. The only other sound was the gentle hum of the air-conditioner from the luxurious campervan next door. I couldn't help but smile as I walked past their master bedroom and heard the rumble of deep snoring coming from within.

Seven hours later, I stepped into glaring sunshine and headed towards the shower block, unwilling to make eye contact with our rested neighbours. A quick glance revealed they were already enjoying coffee under the shade of their wide awning, while reading the morning papers.

The humidity dropped a few days later, just as we'd packed for our next destination, Byron Bay. Our neighbours had similar plans and for a few minutes we stood side by side, unplugging cables and water pipes. I asked about their next destination, but their response was half-hearted, mentioning something about the Gold Coast, so I didn't pry further.

As they revved their engine and manoeuvred the vehicle out of the campsite, I thought over our time in Port Macquarie. Despite the humidity and sleepless nights, it had been rewarding, with early morning yoga sessions on the nearby beach, surfing for the boys and the chance to unwind at a beachside café. Our camp was positioned close to the last stretch of the Hastings River before it met with the South Pacific. All day long, family-sized boats cruised up and down the wide river and anglers stood on the rocks, casting their lines into the deep water.

Most mornings we strolled into town for a coffee or a green smoothie, before returning to our camp. Close by, a coastal walk stretched for nine kilometres, offering the chance to get up high to admire secluded coves of crystal-clear water. There was also the option to divert from the path to spend time on isolated beaches, with a warning on one placard that nudity was prohibited!

The camp kitchen proved to be invaluable, and during a communal barbeque we learned about the local koala hospital. We put this on our list and took a drive after checking out of the campsite on our last morning. The three-hour visit began with a sighting of my first wild koala, resting in the branches of a majestic gum tree on the hospital grounds.

Endearing and treasured, the koala is an iconic marsupial native to Australia, recognised for its cuddly appearance. Sporting a grey coat, fluffy ears, and a cute button-like nose, the koala's irresistible allure has enchanted people around the world. Found mostly in eucalyptus trees, these charming creatures are under threat from habitat loss and during the hospital tour we discovered that many of them had been orphaned because their mothers had been killed by vehicles. Others had survived bush fires, but the injuries sustained meant they could no longer fend for themselves in the wild.

Most koalas were housed in open-plan pens, except for those going through rehabilitation. There was also the chance to adopt a koala and the money raised helps with medical fees, along with the funding of projects to conserve and expand their habitat. The adoption package allows you to select your chosen koala, including a framed photo, along with their story and the chance to learn more about the hospital.

Our boys adopted a koala each and as Fran drove out of the car park, I read about the one that Seby had picked. 'Aussie Mick' no longer lived at the hospital, but being a white koala, instead of the typical greyish brown, meant he was a popular choice. After being diagnosed with an eye infection, he'd made a full recovery, before being released into nearby bushland.

As Fran drove us out of town, we passed a colourful road sign depicting a koala. Despite our search from the car windows, there was no sign of them in the treetops. Before long, we were on a busy freeway, heading north towards our next destination.

By the time we pulled into our campsite near Byron Bay, the sun was dropping towards the tree line. The reception area was clean and cool, the soft drone from its air conditioner the only sound as we waited in line. Leaving Fran to sort out the arrangements, I wandered over to a display of tourist information leaflets. The boys selected flyers for surf schools, kayaking adventures, and movies under the stars. I collected a handful of pamphlets promoting coastal walks, bike hire, and sunset markets.

One thing was obvious–six nights in Byron Bay would never be enough time to experience all it offered. As promised after Fran's earlier call, they'd allocated us a shaded plot. The boys ran ahead with a site map and directed me to a lush bed of grass, surrounded by the kind of trees I'd expected to see in the jungle. Parrots cavorted in the canopies, their constant squawking and playful antics tempting me to grab a camera. After my brush with nature, I got to work on connecting the power and water, humming a song while setting up the outdoor table.

'What are you so happy about?' Fran asked, as she emerged from the campervan with an empty kettle.

'Look at this place–it's perfect. We have sunshine or shade, a pool, a communal barbeque and can even walk to the beach. The humidity has dropped, the birds are singing and the boys are playing cricket. What more do we want?'

'I agree, Ali. I love it already. All I need is a cup of tea and a few bits for dinner. Maybe some lamb chops and salad.'

Just then, Noah called out, 'Mum, can we go to the pool? It's too hot for cricket.'

After one look at their glowing faces, I took the initiative and came up with a plan. 'Fran, you go for a dip, and I'll dash to the shops. When I get back, I'll crank the barbeque and pour the drinks.'

In reply, she looked across the campsite and said, 'It seems weird to be so close to Byron Bay after all these years.'

I held up the van keys and gave them a jangle. 'Maybe you should go shopping instead. I'm happy to swim with the boys.'

'No, that's okay. We can enjoy it all tomorrow. You won't be long, will you?'

'I'll be back before you know it.'

Before setting off, I strolled towards the toilet block and noticed a groundsman inspecting a drain. He was dressed in shorts and a T-shirt, but had opted for comfort rather than safety, discarding sturdy footwear for beach sandals. I stopped for a chat and asked why the caravan park wasn't filled, despite the lovely weather. He looked around and gave a weary smile. 'It's busy enough for me! There'll be loads more people during the weekend and the young ones like to stay in town, where the action is.'

He then looked towards our campervan, where Fran and the boys were preparing for their dip. 'In my opinion, this is the best place to stay. You're only a ten-minute drive from Byron Bay, and you'll probably have the barbeque area to yourself this evening. After dark, you'll hear the sound of frogs and the call of a tawny frogmouth. Know what they are? Not frogs at all, but a bird that looks like an owl.'

While I digested his news, he asked, 'Have you been to Byron Bay before?'

'No, but my wife was here years ago and loved it.'

'She'll find it's changed. It's not all bad, mind you, and there's plenty to do. The beaches are still amazing but it's no longer a sleepy town with a hippy vibe. House prices have gone crazy and every man and his dog from the city wants to live here. Some old-timers have been forced inland, which is a real shame. If you get the chance to try out the Bangalow markets, you'll get a feel of what Byron Bay used to be like.

Now, if you'll excuse me, I'd better unblock this drain before anyone uses the shower.'

If most hippies have moved inland in search of cheaper property, I must have been in luck, as I spotted one on the way to the supermarket. Of course, I have no idea if she was a hippy or not and am conscious that it's a clichéd tag, given without too much thought. But if you believe that anyone with waist-length braided hair, wearing faded dungarees, gumboots, and sporting an array of body art could be a hippy, then we're on the same wavelength. She was riding along the path and her bike even had a wicker basket positioned at the front.

As I came to a stop at a zebra crossing, she lifted a hand in a gesture of acknowledgement while cycling across the road. She looked deeply tanned and had probably been that way for decades, with fine lines etched across her rounded face. After reaching the far side, she darted through an alleyway, leaving the road clear for me to continue my journey.

Ten minutes later I found a supermarket on the outskirts of town and searched for a parking spot, noting the number of other campervans nearby. One looked as though it had just come in from the desert after many months, with scratched paintwork and minor dents across the doors and bonnet. Each scuff mark and bump no doubt had a story behind their inception, either from mishaps with wildlife, other road users, the vegetation or the owners themselves. The rear window of one van was home to a colourful selection of stickers, depicting faraway places such as Alice Springs, Fraser Island and Cape Tribulation, to prove where the vehicle had once been.

Another van looked as though it had just crossed the arid interior, with the dried remains of insects and animal parts splattered across the front grill and bumper. A quick peek inside the rear window gave me an insight into the nomadic lives of the owners, as I noted two wetsuits, sleeping bags, tinned provisions, pots, pans and a portable gas hob. Most other campervans were just like mine–far too shiny and in need of a longer adventure.

After a successful search for provisions, I headed back to the van and started the engine. From the car park, I could have turned right, which would have led me straight back to the campsite. According to an overhead signpost, the left turn looked far more appealing–as the road would take me into the centre of town. As if on autopilot, I took the left turn, navigated a roundabout and found myself in a busy street, lined with people.

Some wandered along the pavements wearing beachwear, but many others were dressed for an evening on the town, sitting on bar stools and sipping drinks while gazing over the street through open windows. I passed intimate bars, tucked alongside restaurants and cafés to suit every taste and budget. Each street corner seemed to have a shop selling surf wear, with colourful placards placed outside, offering surfing lessons for all ages and abilities.

The road led me directly to the bay, where I parked up before strolling towards the beach. To my right I could see the outline of a lighthouse, perched on top of a wooded headland. I knew from our guidebook that a rocky outcrop, just beyond the lighthouse, marked the eastern tip of mainland Australia. Despite the lateness of the day, the beach was still busy, with people lounging on towels and others walking hand in hand along the shoreline.

In the last of the light, I caught sight of a surfer, paddling fast to catch a wave. With apparent ease, she sprung onto the board into a crouching position, her arms out wide, before standing upright. As the board picked up speed, she coasted along the face of the wave, which seemed to loom from the water with every second.

As the wave changed shape and threatened to break, she kicked hard to slice her way back to deeper water. The wave broke soon after, sending sea spray into the air, before rolling towards the golden beach. As I studied the lone surfer, a sudden thought struck me. After all these years in Australia, I'd never tried surfing. Yet here I was, in Byron Bay, close to some of the most popular surf spots in Australia.

During the drive back to our campsite, I decided it was now or never to give the sport a go. I just needed to find out how to organise a lesson. Partway through our barbeque the answer came unexpectedly, in the form of Jerry, who strolled up to the camp kitchen, armed with a handful of advertising flyers.

He was tall and lean, with flyaway hair and a weathered face. While greeting us with handshakes and a wide smile, he handed out flyers and asked the boys if they enjoyed surfing. After receiving nods of approval, he then raised his voice. 'Well, make sure you tell your mum and dad, as I've got a cracking offer for them. I've been surfing for years and if they sign up for a lesson, I'll only charge half price.'

After a scan of her pamphlet, Fran was keen to learn more. 'Where will you take us to surf, Jerry?'

'We'll head to a secret spot where the waves are perfect for any age or ability. I'm telling you now, you'll have the best morning of your life. As for riding a wave, I guarantee each of you will stand on a board before we head home.'

I'd been quiet up to this point, watching and enjoying his animated antics while he tried interacting with our boys. By now they'd moved towards the trees, watching with interest as Jerry turned his attention towards me. 'What about it then, Dad? Are you up for the best morning of your life?'

I smiled and said, 'That's a bold statement, Jerry. I've had a few enjoyable moments so far and—'

Before I could finish, he cut in, while patting me on the back. 'I love the Pommie accent. Cor blimey mate and all of that.'

'I'm not a cockney, Jerry. I'm from a town called Luton, just outside—'

'Whatever, mate, you're still a Pom, but don't worry, we Aussies love you all. Have you surfed before? You look the sporty type.'

'No, but I was thinking of booking a lesson during the week.'

He stuck his hand out, waiting for me to shake it. As I did so, he said, 'Well this is your lucky day, as I've got four spots left for tomorrow. What's your name, mate?'

'I'm Alistair and this is Fran. Our boys are Noah and Seby.'

'Well, Alistair, are you game to give it a go? I just need 50 dollars as a deposit and then I'll leave you in peace to enjoy your lamb chops.'

After pocketing the money, he said, 'I can tell that your boys are as keen as mustard to get on the water. I reckon you'll be a natural as well.'

He left as quickly as he arrived, with a promise to meet in the morning, while dashing towards the roadway with my 50 dollars! Luckily, he was a man of his word and greeted us all with a cheery smile the following morning, as we strolled out of our campsite towards a parking bay. We soon discovered he drove a road-weary minivan, hitched to a trailer filled with surfboards. Once on board, we searched for vacant seats and chatted with the other holidaymakers he'd signed up. They ranged from young families to weekenders and global backpackers, all looking to try surfing for the first time.

During the practice session on a sun-kissed beach, it all looked so easy, even though the hired boards had all seen better days. Each had dents and scars, with some boards held firm by strips of duct tape, like wounded soldiers wrapped in bandages. Jerry's two assistants soon came to the rescue, taking the children in one group and the competent swimmers in another, which also included Fran.

I got put with Jerry and a sprightly couple from Melbourne who'd recently retired and were keen to 'try anything once.' They were true to their word and gave the waves one shot each, before giving up and heading towards a mobile coffee van parked close to shore. Suddenly alone, I had Jerry's full attention. Above the sound of breaking waves, he called out once again. 'As I told you, Alistair. This is going to be the best morning of your life. You'll be riding a wave soon enough. If not, you'll get your money back! Okay, are you ready this time? Here comes another wave!'

Chest-deep in the water, I waded towards the back of the board and pulled myself up, so my stomach lay flat on the foam, with my outstretched hands clutching the sides. As I did so, Jerry steadied the board and called out, 'No, not like that, Alistair. Like I said before, stretch your left leg towards the back and lock the right knee into position.'

After many attempts, I still didn't understand what he was talking about, but made another effort to impress by lying as flat as possible while sliding various body parts across the damp surface. After a quick warning, he pushed the board, so it caught the face of the oncoming wave. As the wave propelled me towards the faraway beach, I heard him yelling out instructions. Sometime soon I was meant to go from lying, to crouching and then to standing. But the timing never seemed to be right and each time I moved, the board spun out of control, resulting in yet another dunking.

The simplest option, I discovered, was to cling to the sides, with my stomach flat on the board, until I'd reached dry land. During the next hour, I lost count of the number of times I went through the same scenario, all with the same disappointing results.

My children were still in the ocean, just beyond the main break, learning advanced techniques from their seasoned instructor. Fran had stood up on her second attempt, prompting loud cheers from those nearby. After a few more successful surfs, she'd also returned to the shallows, her eyes on our children while grasping a camera to capture photos of them tackling distant waves.

Now I was lying flat on the board, heading towards shore, with my thoughts on a late breakfast rather than a return to deeper waters where Jerry still loomed. As the surfboard dragged in the sand, Fran walked towards me, the water swirling around her ankles. 'You didn't even try that time, Ali.'

'I don't care anymore. The wetsuit is baggy, my fingers are numb and I've fallen off too many times. I'm just too old to learn.'

She rolled her eyes and smiled. 'That's a silly statement and you know it.'

She then pointed towards Jerry, standing alone in the surf, waiting for me to return. 'Look, he's trying to get your attention and it's not like you to give up so easily. Go on, give it one more try. The boys would be so proud.'

'To be honest, all I want is a coffee and a croissant from the takeaway van. We've been up for hours. Isn't it time to head back to the campsite?'

While getting to my feet, I searched the distant crests for signs of our boys. I noticed Seby, arms wide, legs bent, surfing a faraway wave. In the blink of an eye, he was tumbling through the air, momentarily lost in the white water before surfacing. Between the swells, I searched for Noah's blonde hair and saw him bobbing on the water alongside his instructor, as they waited for a suitable wave.

Fran cast her gaze towards the ocean and said, 'Look, the boys are having fun and Jerry is waving at you. This could be your moment.'

Like the geeky kid at school who hated sports lessons, I headed back towards my teacher. The swells had grown in stature since our arrival, pounding my upper body with each step into deeper water. As each one tore down, I leapt high, ignoring the earlier advice to duck-dive below them. By now I'd become conditioned to Jerry's booming voice, forever giving advice on how to catch the waves. Maybe it was hunger, a lack of sleep, or just the fact that I didn't care, as nothing made sense anymore. The only thing keeping me in the water was my stubbornness and Jerry's persistence.

I could see in his eyes that the fight was over. He had nothing more to say, and I was beyond listening. As the next set of waves loomed from the water, I called out, 'Jerry, this is my last go, mate. You look like you need a break and I'm ready for a coffee. Please don't tell me what to do this time. Let's see how it goes.'

For once, he was silent, and as the wave approached, I lay down on the board in preparation. Jerry pushed at exactly the right moment, propelling the board towards the beach. This time, I didn't jerk, or waver, or think too deeply. In one motion, I went from lying to crouching, feeling the creamy water spill over my toes.

Then I was standing, my arms wide, and the grin on my face even wider. Fran stood by the water's edge with camera in hand, snapping away, capturing every moment. Unfortunately, her zoom lens was pointed further offshore, where the boys tackled the larger swells. Over the sound of waves breaking on the shore, I heard my voice, mysteriously high-pitched as I fought for her attention. She didn't hear me, but I knew Jerry would be watching from afar. All that mattered was that for a fleeting moment, I was surfing on the east coast of Australia, under a blazing sun.

During the next few days, we explored the area. Sometimes by campervan, other times on foot or on hired bikes.

One Sunday morning we took a 20-minute drive inland, towards the country town of Bangalow. Along the way, we drove through a fertile landscape dotted with trees and farmhouses. During the journey, narrow roads to our left and right offered the chance to explore other communities and towns, hidden behind low-lying hills. Regrettably, we had limited time to explore the back roads and kept our eyes peeled for signs heading to Bangalow.

Held on the fourth Sunday of each month, Bangalow markets have been running since 1982, and as we approached the town, it was clear they hadn't lost their appeal. Cars were parked in every available gap, forcing us towards the quiet side streets to find a space. The unplanned walk gave us the chance to appreciate the leafy neighbourhood, with each house and garden a little different from the next. Some buildings were cute cottages, constructed from timber and painted a dazzling white. Others were grander affairs, with two storeys and views of a nearby creek meandering through woodland.

The main street, with its federation-style buildings, offered a wide selection of cafés and boutique shops. We found the markets a few minutes later, located close to town in a wide paddock, with every type of stall you could wish for. Thousands of people milled around, all enjoying the sunshine at a leisurely pace.

During the next few hours, we treated ourselves to massages and sat with a grey-haired woman, who read our palms and asked for a few dollars. Later, we ate wholesome smoothies, whisked up by a sweet-faced girl who looked like she belonged in San Francisco. In the adjacent field, we discovered a market stall that sold freshly baked pies and ate them while sitting on a bench, listening to a folk band.

While they strummed popular tunes and country classics, barefooted toddlers danced on the grass and parents relaxed in the shade. Sometime later, Fran visited another stall, and came away with henna tattoos on her ankles. Just before leaving, the boys purchased cotton T-shirts and learnt the art of tie-dyeing them.

We draped the damp T-shirts over the back seats of our campervan and headed back to Byron Bay. During the drive, Fran stared out of the windows at the rolling plains and made comments about how green it all looked, compared to the parched countryside that we'd become used to in Western Australia each summer. Finally, she raised her voice and said, 'In many ways, Bangalow reminds me of the Byron Bay I knew long ago.'

She went quiet for a moment, then continued. 'I've really enjoyed our time in Byron Bay, but I hope it doesn't get any bigger or busier. Maybe I need to stay longer next time as it's still a special place for me. By the way, there's one more place I'd like to show you before we fly home. I'll give you a clue. It's white, bright and lights up after dark.'

That afternoon, we hired bikes from the campsite receptionist, with the promise to return them in a few days. The boys decided on a tandem and after a test run around the camp, declared themselves to be experts. Fran then led us towards the lighthouse, which stands at Cape Byron, the easternmost point of the mainland.

We stopped along the way, sometimes to drink water and once for photos, to capture the sweeping views from the peninsula. Far to our right, we could see the deep blue ocean, its rollers crashing onto a serene stretch of sand, fringed by a subtropical forest. As expected, the lighthouse was painted a brilliant white, but wasn't as tall as I'd hoped. It didn't need to be, due to its prime location at the top of a headland. Visitors milled around its base, some taking photos, while others sat quietly, waiting for a tour guide.

After parking the bikes, we joined a coastal footpath leading away from the lighthouse, offering panoramic views of the surrounding ocean. Along the way, we studied information signs and learned that it's possible to spot humpback whales during their annual migration. We'd missed the spectacle by a few months, but were soon rewarded with sightings of other sea creatures.

We stopped by a barrier and peered into the crystal-clear waters. A pod of dolphins caught our attention, surfing a faraway break, and far below we spotted a juvenile shark patrolling the shallows. Further on, the path dipped and the trees thinned, until we arrived close to the water's edge.

Far in the distance, two small islands peeking from the water signified our first sighting of Julian Rocks. No doubt, Captain James Cook would once have spotted these two rounded outcrops during his epic adventure on the research vessel, *HMS Endeavour*. An excerpt from one of his journals captures the moment that he sailed past these shores, on the 15th May, 1770.

'A tolerable high point of land bore Northwest by West, distance three miles; this point I named Cape Byron.'

He named the area after Captain John Byron, one of his predecessors, who'd circumnavigated the world in *HMS*

Dolphin, between 1764 and 1766. The waters surrounding the rocks are now a marine sanctuary, where you'll find grey nurse sharks and three different species of turtle, along with manta rays and huge schools of pelagic fish, including barracuda and mackerel.

We turned our eyes back to the narrowing path, now etched into a jut of land. The trees had gone, replaced by soft grass and a welcome breeze. We strode onwards until there was nowhere else to go. We'd arrived at the most eastern point of mainland Australia. Each of us found a pebble, and before returning to the lighthouse we threw them into the wind and watched as they bounced off the rocks and dropped into the ocean.

On our last day, we headed to the beach at Byron Bay. Fran left us for a while, to wander the streets and laneways. She returned hours later, lost in thought, while carrying a paper bag filled with trinkets and mementos. She'd also found another surf school and had booked the boys into an afternoon lesson. The instructor was in his mid-twenties, wide shouldered, with deep green eyes and long brown hair, styled into dreadlocks. He greeted the boys with a smile and as they shook hands, he asked them their names.

I recognised his accent at once and guessed correctly that he was from County Donegal, in the northwest of Ireland. In recent years, Donegal's surfing scene has grown in stature and the seaside town of Bundoran has also hosted the European surfing championships. After learning his trade in the cool waters of the Atlantic Ocean, Michael was now living the dream, sharing his skills and experience with visitors from across the world. He helped the boys select a suitable board, along with wetsuits, before we all walked across the road to the beach.

Along the way, I was keen to chat about Donegal and mentioned the name of the town where my mum had grown up. He knew it well and had once enjoyed a pint of Guinness in my uncle's pub, known as the Corner House. But he wasn't in the mood for reminiscing, as he had two boys by his side, eager to learn a few valuable tips.

After two hours of tuition, the boys emerged from the ocean with weary smiles on their faces. We thanked Michael with a tip for a well-earned drink and then headed home to prepare for our last evening in Byron Bay. After showering, we made our way to the campervan, but on impulse I pointed towards our hired bikes. 'Who'd like to cycle into town instead?'

Minutes later, we were cycling along a footpath towards town, merrily chatting away about our day. As the boys took the lead, both giving instructions on how best to ride a tandem, Fran pedalled close to me, the smile on her face the widest I'd seen in years.

I can't compare the old Byron Bay to the present one, but found it to be a memorable location. It's the kind of coastal town where hippies brush shoulders with weekenders, who come in search of tapas, acoustic sounds and a sunset view for happy hour. It's also the kind of place where skateboarders ride through the town centre at dusk, overtaking queues of cars, mile-weary VW campers and shiny Range Rovers.

The golden beach attracts all types of people from all walks of life. Some, like me, are happy to read a book between brave attempts at surfing or body boarding. Others take to the water for hours, tackling the famous surf breaks that helped put Byron Bay on the map many years ago. It's the kind of town where two boys can cycle down the busy streets towards the Pacific Ocean at sunset and not turn a head. Even though they're wearing tie-dye T-shirts, giggling loudly and riding a tandem.

A Place in the Sun

"It's summer and time for wandering..."
– Kellie Elmore

Living so close to the ocean, in a coastal town that attracts thousands of visitors each summer, it would have made sense to stay put for Christmas. The southwest corner of Western Australia boasts world-class wineries, family-friendly caravan parks, microbreweries set in rolling farmland, ancient forests and epic surf breaks. The white sandy beaches are lapped by warm, clear water, which in places is teeming with fish. Hidden coves and protected bays offer idyllic swimming conditions, and those who enjoy fishing can cast a line from a myriad of stunning locations.

Despite having so much on offer close to my doorstep, I still felt the urge to get out of town for Christmas. So, one November morning, I decided to give our camper trailer a spring clean. My first impression was not a good one, as it had been standing forgotten for many months at the bottom of the garden. Weeds had sprouted underneath the rusted suspension and each tyre looked deflated and worn. Further investigation revealed an ant's nest in the kitchenette, along with a leaky canvas.

I'd been sold a dream a few years earlier, believing the camper would be perfect for spontaneous weekends away with the family. We'd tried it out a few times, with little success. The first time, we camped at a municipal site in a nearby forest and our boys were bursting with excitement after finishing school early.

After unhitching the camper, we followed the detailed instructions from the previous owner, a family friend who was keen for an upgrade. During the exchange of money and paperwork, he'd advised us to study the information and his parting words had made us all smile. 'Be sure to pitch the camper on level ground, as you don't want to be rolling out of bed on your first night.'

This task sounded simple enough until we discovered that the last remaining spot for our camper was a lumpy patch of sand, close to a line of peppermint trees. We soon learned why the main compartment of the camper was home to various pieces of flat timber, and we put them to use on the uneven ground to help stabilise the wheels. After copious amounts of pushing and pulling, the questions started pouring from my two young helpers.

'Dad, shouldn't the camper be facing the other way?'

'Dad, shouldn't we be following the next instruction? It says you have to let the tyres down in sandy conditions.'

Instead of watching me falter, Fran's eyes were on our neighbours, sitting outside their camper while enjoying cool drinks. 'Why don't we ask that couple over there? Their set-up looks just perfect...'

Two weeks later, as we arrived at a riverside setting and began setting up camp, the questions poured forth once again.

'Dad, didn't we point the camper away from the trees last time?'

'Dad, did you remember to pack the instructions?'

'Do you want a cold beer?' Fran asked quietly. 'You look a little stressed.'

Once the ground was levelled, the real feat of endurance involved heaving the canvas from its housing. It was then pulled tight, with each family member holding a corner, while the poles were inserted in sequence. If the poles had been numbered or colour coded, life would have been easier.

Some had once been marked up, but the numbers had smudged over time and in the heat of the day, made little sense. Instead, they ranged in length, width, and weight, creating various contorted shapes as the poles were swapped around.

Weekends away in the camper were put on hold, but each summer we rolled it out of the garage for week-long holidays. Even these seemed too short, when considering the time to set up and take down afterwards. We eventually ignored the camper altogether and booked into chalets or rental apartments instead.

I tried selling it on eBay a few times, but those who came to view it made silly offers. Instead, their focus was on the shinier models flooding the market, imported from China in vast quantities. I'd heard horror stories about them falling apart when put to the test, and doubted they could compare with the robust design of my camper, which had been built to handle off-road tracks.

Faced with a lack of buyers, I decided to overhaul the camper to its original condition. All it needed was a few new parts and some focused attention. It might not be ideal for weekends away, but would be okay for a week or more, when we had more time to play with the poles. Maybe one more road trip would rekindle the wanderlust I'd felt after buying it so many years earlier.

During a recent trip to Perth, I'd picked up a brochure on Kalbarri, brought to life by glossy photos and vivid descriptions of its many attractions on the mid-west coast of Australia. It had been many years since our last visit and I'd forgotten about the Murchison River, which cuts through the edge of town before taking a dogleg towards the Indian Ocean.

With a catchment area greater than Tasmania and a total length of 820 kilometres, the river sounded impressive and I was keen to paddle along the final stretch before it reaches the ocean. This same river is responsible for the steep gorges further inland, formed by erosion over millions of years, creating a series of natural viewpoints which overlook clear pools of water, far below.

The back pages of the brochure listed activities on offer, including bush-tucker tours, fishing charters, canoe safaris and wilderness cruises. It also featured quad biking, abseiling, and other outdoor pursuits. Kalbarri sounded the perfect family getaway over Christmas, especially as we were due a visit from my adventurous big brother, who was keen to escape from the grey skies of an English winter.

But if such a holiday was to take place, I needed to repair the camper trailer first. The trip would take about ten hours by car, and with only a month to go until Christmas, we hadn't even booked a camping spot. Besides, I still hadn't talked to Fran and the boys. They'd be sure to think I was crazy to suggest we travel so far north, when we had so many options close to our doorstep.

Yet something about revisiting Kalbarri had captured my imagination. Maybe it was the chance to enjoy watching the resident pelicans or to laze away the hours on a nearby beach while throwing in a fishing line. Either way, I felt it was time to get out of town for a while.

Thousands of visitors would soon descend on our south-west hometown, but with any luck, we'd be heading in the opposite direction. That evening, while we lounged outside, I called for a moment's silence. The boys were lying together in the hammock and Fran was nearby, reading a magazine.

'Listen up everyone. I've got an idea about Christmas. I think we should go camping in Kalbarri.'

It was Fran who replied first, her eyes peering over the magazine. 'Sounds like fun to me, but I didn't think you liked the camper anymore. The last time we went away, you vowed to sell it as soon as possible!'

'I did try, but no one was interested. Anyway, I've been reading about Kalbarri, and I reckon it will be a perfect place to try the camper one more time, especially during the holidays. Busselton and the whole of the southwest will be packed solid in a few weeks. Every man and his dog from Perth will appear with their boats, mountain bikes and fishing rods. The cafés will be mobbed, with queues at the supermarkets and cars parked everywhere.'

As I reeled off a list of complaints, Fran let out a chuckle. 'Oh, you are funny. This is nothing compared to what we left behind in the UK, with the crowds and traffic jams all year round. Australians are used to big road trips and the change of scenery will do us good.'

She then asked the boys, 'What do you two think?'

'Can we watch movies in the car?' Noah asked.

'Yes, of course,' I replied, with little thought about how Fran might react. The cool stare told me her position, and she had the last word. 'Have you worked out how we'll get a camping spot so close to Christmas? *And* your brother will be here on holiday.'

'Dave won't mind. He'll just be glad to get away from an English winter and can use our two-man tent.'

'Look, it's up to you, Ali. You're the one most in need of a holiday and it's *your* brother who's arriving soon. But if you want us to go, then you'd better see if there's a vacancy first.'

The following morning, I called the campsites in Kalbarri. I got lucky on the third attempt, thanks to a recent cancellation. The site had a family-friendly pool, a communal kitchen and barbeque area. After confirming the booking, I turned my attention to the leaky canvas, in case we were caught out with a summer downpour. With new tyres, greased bearings and a squirt of WD40 in every nook and cranny, the camper was soon spruced up and ready to go.

Dave arrived as planned, and after sleeping off his jetlag in our hammock, soon made himself at home. He'd been to Australia many times before, including a trip to Kalbarri. The following day, I asked if he minded going again and his chirpy reply was as expected. 'As long as it's sunny, I don't care where we go. Last time I went, I caught a dhufish.'

I eased out a smile and watched as he scrolled through his phone to find a photo. It didn't take long, just a minute or two, but during that time, I thought back to all the times I'd tried catching a decent sized fish. Fourteen years in Australia and I'd not caught anything bigger than a pilchard.

The reputation of the dhufish isn't just related to their size, although the largest can grow up to a metre and weigh as much as 25 kilograms. They are a sought-after, tasty specimen and are known to put up a fight! To help preserve stocks for the future, fisheries have introduced strict quotas on bag limits and size, which means they are becoming a rare catch.

Dave turned his phone around for me to see the picture. As expected, he looked delighted. Months of travel had tanned his face, as he stood on the open deck of a fishing boat while holding aloft his prized catch.

'You call that a fish?' I said, before adding, 'That's the kind of thing I use for bait nowadays.'

'I didn't know you were keen on deep-sea fishing,' he said.

'There's a lot you don't know about me, Dave. It's been a few years since you've been here, and I've had lots of time for practice. Maybe we'll try our luck in Kalbarri.'

Fran must have overheard the conversation, and as he walked away, she called me to one side. 'What are you saying, Ali? You can hardly tie a knot on a hook, let alone catch a prize fish.'

'Yes, but he doesn't know that yet. Anyway, it'll keep him on his toes for a few days, wondering if I've ever caught a bigger fish than he has.'

Dave offered to be the first to drive, and we left at dawn for Kalbarri on the Saturday before Christmas, with a ten-hour journey in front of us. For the first few hours, we drove north along an empty highway, but as we neared the outskirts of Perth, the traffic in the opposite direction steadily increased, as though there'd been a mass evacuation of the city. Some vehicles had trailers attached, filled with scooters, portable barbeques, children's bikes, tents and fishing rods.

We drove uninterrupted towards the city skyline and passed over the wide expanse of the Swan River. To our left stood a lofty swathe of greenery, signalling Kings Park, covering 400 hectares and renowned as one of the most spectacular inner-city parks in the world. Soon we were free from the city centre, travelling towards the northern suburbs, an urban sprawl that sits close to the coastline.

The freeway heading south was filling fast, as cars of every type appeared on various slipways and junctions to join the exodus. Some vehicles towed caravans, and many more carried their bikes and surfboards on roof racks. After breaking free of the northern suburbs, we joined the Brand Highway, which is not so much a highway as a long stretch of dual carriageway.

An hour north of Perth we passed signs for Gingin, one of the oldest rural towns in Western Australia. There are many claims to how the town got its name, with most locals agreeing that it means 'a place of many streams.'

If there were streams nearby, they went unnoticed as the winding road led us through gaps in the low-lying hills. The settlements to our left were close to the Indian Ocean, with appealing names such as Seabird and Ledge Point. The roads that headed inland led towards an area known as the Wheatbelt. This premium agricultural region is spread over thousands of kilometres and is where most of Western Australia's crops are grown, including wheat, barley, oats and canola.

In spring, the Wheatbelt bursts into life, as wildflowers carpet the roadside and adjacent meadows. During this period, thousands of weekenders flock to the countryside to admire the natural kaleidoscope of colours and in doing so, help to rejuvenate the remote towns and communities. Now, during the height of summer, the meadows would be parched, with fewer visitors heading inland.

Occasionally, we overtook four-wheel-drive vehicles towing caravans or boats. Some caravan owners displayed their names on the rear of the vans, along with the frequency on which to call them. Without a two-way radio, all we could do was wave while driving past, although I'm sure they'd have been fun to talk to.

Bob and Sheila. Spending the kids inheritance. UHF 18.
Verna and Wayne. A long way from Melbourne. UHF 18.
Big Daz and Little Suzy. Grey Nomads Rule. CH 10.

Near the small town of Eneabba, we stopped at a roadhouse for the chance of food and to stretch our legs and fill up with fuel. Roadhouses are found throughout rural Australia and can be a lifeline for those on long trips through sparsely populated areas. Some offer little more than fuel pumps, toilets and the chance of a takeaway snack. Others have additional facilities, including cabins, camping spots and gas-powered showers. They also sell the basics such as bread, milk and the daily newspaper.

I've often wondered how far some Australians will travel each day to shop for fresh milk and a newspaper. There must be a point when it's just not worth the effort. But if there's one thing I've learned from my time in Australia, those that live away from the city are used to long road trips. In a country close to the size of continental USA, it's just a way of life.

Limbs stretched, bellies full and fuel tank replenished, it was time to be on the move once again. With the air conditioner cranked, I drove out of the service station and stopped by the white line to study the highway. The boys were complaining about flies in the back, but my mind was on other matters. A vehicle was approaching from the left, its bright headlights far from the ground. Seconds later, it rumbled past, leaving a cloud of red dust in its wake. Dave had noticed and called out, 'Boys, are you looking? There goes the first road train of the trip.'

Australia is home to the longest and heaviest road trains in the world, some of which are over 50 metres long. When loaded, they can weigh up to 200 tonnes and are used for the transportation of many goods, including grain, fuel, iron ore and chemicals. When driving through industrial estates, I've often seen signs on the back of trucks, saying *Without Trucks, Australia Stops.*

Vast tracts of rural Australia are devoid of train lines, which means the country relies heavily on its network of roads and haulage trucks to move goods between towns, cities and remote communities. Some road trains travel interstate, covering many thousands of kilometres to deliver essential supplies.

I'd done my homework on road trains and discovered that their drivers are some of the most courteous people you are likely to meet on the road. Over the years, an unofficial etiquette has developed between the regulars on the highways and the drivers of oversized vehicles. Using UHF radios and vehicle indicators, some drivers communicate with each other to ensure they can safely overtake. Of course, there's nothing safer than looking for yourself before deciding to drive along the wrong side of a road to pass a very long vehicle!

We soon caught up with the road train, which had slowed due to a gradual incline. The road ahead was dead straight and devoid of oncoming traffic. Just as I'd inched from the left lane, Dave informed me the road train was signalling. Did this mean it was about to turn? Or was the driver giving me a signal to carry on past?

With no side roads in sight, I eased into the right-hand lane and accelerated. My hands gripped the steering wheel as we drove alongside the mass of steel, its many wheels nearly as tall as our car. If I'd been a passenger, I might have counted the number of wheels we passed. But I was responsible for many lives and kept my eyes on the long straight road ahead. I've no idea how long it took me to overtake, but it felt like an eternity.

Was it my imagination or could I see headlights in the distance? I pushed the accelerator towards the floor and sped ahead of the juggernaut. I was conscious of pulling in too quickly, so I stayed in the right-hand lane until my camper trailer was way ahead of the extra-long vehicle. Like giant tankers in the ocean, road trains appreciate an easy passage and an open road. After returning to the left lane, I felt the tension in my arms begin to ease and searched the road ahead. I'd been right about the faraway headlights. It was another road train, thundering towards us.

In the split second it passed by, I caught sight of the driver, his hand raised in a wave. His greeting was directed at the road train driver 100 metres behind me. Maybe they also chatted on the UHF radio, sharing information about road conditions, weather forecasts, and families on holiday while towing camper trailers! Not long after, the road dipped and curved and I overtook another road train. This time, a designated passing lane made for a calmer experience.

Before reaching the coastal city of Geraldton, we stopped by the Greenough Flats for the chance to take photos of unusual gum trees. A designated layby offered us a safe place to stretch our legs and admire the nearest tree. Normally, such a specimen would grow at least twenty metres tall, but its lower trunk was bent at right angles, causing most of the tree to trail across the ankle high scrub.

It looked to me as though the tree had been beaten into submission by the wind throughout its life, with no chance to stand proud. A weathered placard gave a few clues to the unusual phenomenon, including the salty air that blows from the ocean, across the flats, burning off growth on the windward side of each tree.

Dave was keen to drive again, and I was happy to let him take the lead. Two hours later, we arrived on the outskirts of Kalbarri and took an opportune detour along a lonely coastal road. After parking on a clifftop, we strolled towards a lookout point to admire the choppy stretch of water below. We'd arrived at Pot Alley, so called because of the potted holes etched into the steep bluff walls.

From up high the water looked a sparkling blue, fringed by limestone reefs that prove a perfect habitat for sea life, including lobsters. Rock lobsters are big business in the Midwest, and the quotas are managed to ensure sustainability for the future. It's estimated that the Midwestern rock lobster industry contributes 500 million dollars to the state's economy each year. Before heading back to the car, we searched for fishing boats out at sea and spotted a few, dotted amongst the whitecaps.

After passing the *Welcome to Kalbarri* sign, we found our campsite easily enough. Along the way, we drove alongside a convenience store, a camping shop, two pubs, a selection of cafés and a two-storey restaurant offering ocean views from an upper balcony. The river was to our left, sprinkled with boats, and close by, families played on a sandbank, enjoying the afternoon sunshine.

After paying the remainder of our camping fee, we were given a site map and informed about the golden rule–to drive slowly and safely around the site. There were children everywhere, from toddlers to teenagers. Some were on scooters and bikes, others on foot, while in transit to or from the open-air pool, which looked to be in high demand. On first impressions, each camping spot looked spacious, with enough room between tents and caravans to allow for a semblance of privacy. Each plot was numbered, and we'd booked a powered site, along with a water supply fed by a communal standpipe.

The first caravan we passed had a Christmas tree outside, decorated with twinkling fairy lights. Many other holidaymakers were also in the Christmas spirit, with displays of tinsel a common sight across the frontage of tents and caravans. One tent even had a life-sized snowman outside, just waiting to be inflated.

As soon as we'd parked by our allocated plot, the boys rummaged around for bathers and set off towards the pool. Fran followed close by, calling for them to apply the sunscreen tucked up with their towels and water bottles. Dave was the next to disappear, in search of the communal toilet.

Suddenly alone, I felt a wave of anxiety as I studied our allocated patch of turf and waved away the flies. With many hours until sunset, there was ample enough time to erect the camper, but somehow the timing seemed wrong. Apart from children at play, there was no one else within sight exerting any energy. Those with any sense were cooling off in the pool or sitting in the shade, enjoying ice-cold drinks. As I reached for my water bottle, a man called out from the camping spot next door. 'Long drive was it, mate?'

The first thing I noticed about him was his rounded belly, hidden behind a stretched singlet. He was lounging in a chair, under the shade of an awning, which formed a part of his off-road touring caravan. I waved and stepped a little nearer. 'Yes, we've been on the road all day, changing drivers every few hours. I'll be ready for a cold beer once the camper is up.'

'Have you used it before?' he asked.

'A few times, but not for a while.'

He then nudged the woman sitting alongside him, before reaching out and selecting two drinks from a nearby fridge. They both altered their seats, to get a better view of my camper. In unison, they cracked opened their cans, took a slurp each and raised them high. The man's voice deepened as he bellowed, 'Off you go then, mate. Our TV is on the blink and we're in need of some entertainment!'

Just as Dave appeared, they turned away to continue their card game, prompting me to note which tent pegs to remove after midnight if they continued with the wisecracks!

Dave then studied the patch of grass we'd rented, before casting his eyes over the camper. 'Ali, I'm sure you're an expert at this, but if I were you, I'd spin the camper around to face away from your neighbours. If we get cracking, we'll be done in no time.'

Fran and the boys soon appeared on the scene, refreshed after their swim and happy to help with pulling out the canvas and tightening the ropes. We even found the time to colour code and number each pole!

In the end, it was the heat that dictated our pace. Occasionally, the boys were dispatched to fill up water bottles. They were also given an errand to head into town for ice creams. By the time they returned, the ice creams were melting, but we were close to the end, with smiles all around. Finally, we'd transformed the camper into our home, including a wraparound awning held tight by tent pegs. In comparison, Dave's tent took all of ten minutes to erect.

In celebration, we opened our first cold drinks and toasted the hazy sunset. We were just in time to watch a family of kangaroos bounce past in search of the newly watered grass which glistened alongside the playground. To complete the day, we strolled into town and ate fish and chips by the riverbank. As we watched anglers cast into the water, the moon made its appearance, low in the sky.

During the holiday, the mercury climbed into the mid-thirties and we soon learned to stay out of the sun during the peak of day. Most mornings we drove a short distance to a protected lagoon known as Blue Holes. As waves crashed onto the outer reef, we snorkelled in the calm waters and searched for butterfly fish, sponges, crustaceans and seagrass.

Later, we'd try one of the many cafés, to enjoy leisurely lunches while waiting for the sun to slide. Mornings were best for kayaking on the river, and sunsets ideal for fishing from the nearby stretch of sand known as Chinaman's Beach.

Sometimes the pelicans paddled close to the beach to investigate our fishing lines, before setting off downstream. One pelican, braver than the others, waddled onto the sand-bank one afternoon, watching us as we fished. Up close, I could appreciate the bright yellow circles around each of its deep black eyes. As the sun dropped lower, the fish began to bite, and soon we were landing feisty herrings. A routine then followed. Two fish for the bucket and one for the pelican, only three steps away, its flesh-pink bill wide open in anticipation.

Occasionally, we headed out of camp for the riverside walk to the pelican feeding station. The daily ritual started in the 1970s, when a local called Cliff Ross began feeding the pelicans with scraps of fish, left over from his early morning catch. If he didn't arrive at the foreshore by a certain time, they sometimes walked or flew across the road and waited by his front door.

Although he has since passed away, his legacy continues, with a team of volunteers taking turns to feed the pelicans. The feeding now takes place on the foreshore each morning, close to where Cliff once lived. This isn't breakfast, but a tasty morsel and a perfect opportunity for the volunteers to check if the pelicans are in good health.

We arrived early on the first morning and grabbed a spot under a shade sail. Wooden seats were positioned in a half circle and as they filled with visitors three pelicans waddled into view. Most children ignored the seats, opting to stand at the front as the pelicans inched closer. Thirty metres away, early morning bathers, paddleboarders and kayakers played in the calm waters of the river.

Although the volunteers have set days, they are flexible enough to swap and change, to ensure the tourists are always treated to an interactive and enjoyable experience. The oldest is Joyce, in her eighties and still going strong. Then there is Brian and Joan, a retired couple, eager to please and happy to answer questions. To complete the picture, Jenny runs the Facebook page, Joe orders the fish, and Felicity stays close to the action, helping and advising when not working as a marriage celebrant.

Felicity arrived at the foreshore by bicycle, with a cheery smile, a small bucket of bait fish and a container for gold coin donations. A few of the pelicans seemed to know her well, jostling for position as excited children stood in line to each receive a fish.

By now, we'd been joined by other pelicans, swooping into view from the river before landing on the sand. Felicity went first and threw a fish to the back, which was scooped up in an instant by a pelican. She then encouraged the children to follow suit, their wayward throws causing laughter from the crowd as gulls swept in to snatch any unclaimed morsels. Felicity then turned her attention to some of the adult spectators and let them have a go at throwing fish to the furthest pelicans. They also enjoyed a tasty treat, and once again, the gulls were quick to scavenge.

During the feeding session, she shared her love of Kalbarri and offered advice and tips about special places for the visitors to experience. She also explained that the gold coin donations not only pay for the pelican's food but also go back to the community. Over the years, the funds have helped pay for school equipment, seasonal festivals and to purchase supplies for the local first-aid volunteers.

During the following days, I learned that each volunteer at the feeding station had their own unique style. Some were quieter and others so chatty that the pelicans waddled forward, getting nearer to the bucket of fish with every step. Most volunteers carried a basic first-aid kit, including a sharp knife and a pair of pliers, which are used to remove fishing lines and hooks from distressed birds.

Conscious of budget, but keen to explore the surrounding area, we picked two organised tours for the week. The first was a canoe trip down the Murchison River, which offered the chance to paddle down the wide, muddy waters on a self-guided expedition.

We were driven to the launch site by one of the local guides, a man named Adrian, who greeted us with a joke and firm handshakes. The 30-minute trip along a sandy track gave the boys plenty to smile about, as Adrian's four-wheel drive vehicle bounced across the rutted track. Up ahead, we spotted kangaroos, startled by the noise and soon running for cover towards the surrounding trees.

The track stopped at an area known as Gregory Rocks, and one by one we unloaded the canoes from the trailer, before placing them in the shallows. In the quiet confines, I rested against a slab of rock as Adrian handed out safety jackets and gave a safety brief. The current would lead us downstream and we needed to sit at all times, with two people in one canoe and three in the other. He then waved us off and watched as we paddled back towards Kalbarri.

There was only one way to go, and the sun was still low in the morning sky. There was also an added bonus, as the flies were yet to discover us. Dave and the boys sat in the front canoe, and I watched as they paddled downstream, carving through the placid water with ease. For a moment, I lay my paddle across the canoe and let my fingers trail in the murky water, feeling a sense of calm as Fran sat ahead, asking why we were falling behind.

It was Fran that spotted the feral goats, watching us from a rocky ridge before scampering away. Soon after, we paddled close to the riverbank and came across two kangaroos, lying in the shade of paperbark trees. As we approached, they lifted their heads to investigate, their ears perked. Within seconds, we'd continued past and they watched us go with disinterest.

By mid-morning, we followed our noses, as the smell of grilled bacon wafted on the breeze. This hastened our paddling as we came around a bend to discover Adrian, waving from the riverbank. He'd cooked enough for a small army, not a family of five, but the barbeque breakfast was very welcome. Afterwards, we boarded the canoes for the last leg. Once again, Adrian pointed downriver and promised to be there to meet us.

The sun was higher now and the flies had found us. In places, the river widened and we watched pelicans scoop the shallows. Along this stretch of river there were a handful of small aluminium boats, powered by outboard motors. They are known as *tinnies* and their owners waved from afar, as they went in search of fishing spots, and we scanned ahead for signs of Adrian.

With perfect timing, we came to a gentle curve in the river and spotted his vehicle and trailer. After packing away the canoes we decided on a swim, and soon discovered that the darkened sand was perfect as an all-over sunscreen. The boys plastered me from head to toe before running away as I gave chase. Their pace was quicker than mine and as they raced into the river and swam towards the centre, it struck me they were no longer youngsters. Moments like these were becoming rare and I savoured their shrieks and laughter, as they called for me to join them.

Days later, we tried our hand at abseiling in Kalbarri National Park, located 30 minutes out of town by car. We were informed by our guides to be there by seven in the morning, because of the high temperatures forecast for the day. Within our group were many nationalities, from countries including Spain, Taiwan, Australia and England. The youngest participant was Sebastian, just eleven, and the oldest was Dave, approaching sixty. Most of the overseas visitors looked to be in their mid-twenties, talking in a mix of languages as we were kitted out with harnesses, protective helmets and gloves.

As our two chirpy guides, Colin and Matt, completed their safety brief, I could feel the heat of the day beginning to build. Although we were seated in an undercover area, the sky above was deep blue and cloudless. Before heading into the nearest gorge, they checked each of us to ensure that we carried enough water and had applied sunscreen.

After a thumbs up, they led us away from the national park entrance towards the gorges. Despite the early start, I could already feel sweat trickling down my neck. The trail was rocky in places but not steep enough to hold anyone back, and we soon formed a single file. Along the way, we stopped to study fossilised tracks in the sandstone, left by ancient sea scorpions, known as eurypterids. These extinct arthropods once grew to two metres and were one of the first creatures known to have walked across the land.

Further on, we came to a high vantage point known as the Z Bend. It offered panoramic views of the gorge and the winding river, far below us. Winter rains were now a distant memory, but pools of water remained, glistening in the early sunlight. Away from the river, the terrain looked parched, except for spindly trees and hardy shrubs, clinging to life amongst the nooks and crannies of the gorge wall.

We spent most of the morning by a series of shady overhangs, chaperoned at all times by Colin and Matt. Throughout this time, their expertise and quick-witted jokes put most of us at ease. In fact, the entire group tackled the longest overhang of all, a sheer-faced 35-metre drop-off.

Watching Noah and Seby, I felt a surge of pride as they took on each new challenge, making sure to impress their uncle from England. In contrast, the Spanish girls screamed in fear during their controlled 35-metre descent, followed by claps and cheers from onlookers as they reached the bottom.

Later, we walked into the belly of the gorge, welcoming the chance to swim in one of the natural pools. The water was refreshingly cold and crystal clear and deep enough to jump in from the sides. Both the Spanish girls yelled out while star-jumping into the water, their shrilled voices echoing across the canyon. Others posed for photos as they lay in the shallows, surrounded by steep walls of sandstone. They also tried getting a signal on their phones to post on Instagram, but in such a location there was no chance.

For a while, all was silent as each of us found a place to relax. The boys swam multiple lengths before searching for rock pools and calling for Fran to watch as they jumped in from a granite ledge, each attempting to get as far as possible. I joined them soon after, but couldn't jump as far or swim as fast. At last, Fran brought me to my senses, offering a bottle of water as I slumped in the shade to admire their antics.

While traipsing out of the gorge, the pace dwindled as the overhead sun sapped our strength. I mentioned ice creams, to cajole the children to the top. By the time we reached the car park, each one of our group was drenched in sweat. Just before we departed, a hired vehicle drove into view and parked up. Each person who got out wore closed-in shoes, long-sleeved shirts and wide-brimmed hats. By starting so late in the day their experience would be different to ours, but thankfully they carried plenty of water.

With one day left in Kalbarri, it was time to head out to sea. A few days earlier, Dave awoke in his two-man tent and found a gift from Santa. Inside, was a voucher for a deep-sea fishing trip and I was to be his chaperone. On our last morning, with promises to bring home dinner, we tiptoed out of camp towards our vehicle for the short drive to the marina.

It was still dark when we stepped on board the 15-metre vessel and met with the crew and additional passengers. Safety brief over, the engines kicked into life as the deckhand passed around bread rolls filled with eggs and bacon, washed down with tea or coffee. We then set off downstream, passing the waking town just to our left. The skipper steered us through the dogleg that leads to the ocean, known as the Kalbarri Gap. Once committed, he powered up the engines and aimed between the markers, which warned of treacherous rocks and sandbars on either side.

We watched the sun rise above the land as we turned south, and the boat cruised through the water towards Pot Alley. A week had passed since I'd stood on the cliffs, gazing at the ocean and watching for boats. Now I was on a fishing charter, hoping to catch a dhufish but suddenly queasy despite the light winds.

As I gripped the railing and took deep breaths, a group of passengers began passing around cold beers! They wore long-sleeved shirts, emblazoned with fishing logos, and as they sipped on early morning drinks, I discovered they were avid fishermen, enjoying a play day away from their partners.

Each had an expensive rod and reel, hooked up in preparation for a prize fish or two. They looked to be in their late twenties with talk about young families and time off work from the mines. As the boat picked up speed, one of them offered me a beer, which I declined with a smile, while fighting the urge to vomit over the side. Instead, I made my excuses and dashed inside for the toilet. As my stomach heaved, the boat pitched and engines roared.

Sometime later, all was quiet. The engine idled, the boat lolled, and laughter sounded from afar. As I stepped outside the toilet and climbed the steps into bright sunshine, a row of fishermen had their backs to me, including Dave. I spotted a flash of colour as he pulled in a fish. It looked larger than anything I'd ever caught in my life. Was it a dhufish? I couldn't be sure, but before I could investigate, my stomach churned, as bile rose to my throat.

I dashed to the toilet with seconds to spare, now aware of the ritual that was to follow and oblivious to the amusement of the fishermen. Sometime later, I found a cramped downstairs bedroom, which included a porthole. Maybe it was the skipper's bed–I didn't ask, but lay my head down and listened to the ocean lapping against the hull.

I woke hours later, in need of water, and made my way towards the deck. Standing in the bright sunshine, I spotted Dave, holding another large fish while asking the deckhand to take a photo. Behind him, the ocean stretched into the distance, with no sight of land. While I sagged against the doorframe and sipped from a water bottle, he smiled and asked me to join him.

I managed a wave but remained in the shade, listening to stories about sharks, dolphins and the fish that got away. One of the younger fishermen passed me on his way to the toilet, asking if I was okay while placing his empty beer bottle alongside a stash of many others.

Ten hours after leaving the marina, the boat sped back through the Kalbarri Gap. Fran and the boys stood on the headland, waving to get our attention as I stood at the stern with Dave. Despite all efforts, he didn't catch a dhufish that day, but pulled in many other species, ranging in size and colour. He captured each moment on his phone, and one day soon, I'll ask him to send me the pictures.

On our last morning, we packed away the camper trailer. Somehow it seemed easier than before, maybe because Dave was on hand to assist, or because the couple from next door were watching and I felt determined to make it look easy. Before leaving Kalbarri, we stopped at the bakery for takeaway pies and then headed to Jakes Point to watch surfers in action. A coffee van was parked alongside the beach, enjoying a brisk trade in the early sunshine. We should have been on the road south by now, but nobody seemed in a hurry to leave. Instead, we sipped drinks and finished our savoury snacks while staring out at the waves.

I hope Kalbarri preserves its magical appeal, as it proved to be a wonderful location for a family friendly holiday, bringing us close together by being close to nature. Nothing stays the same forever, and a Skywalk is planned for construction at the top of the gorge, with two cantilevered viewing platforms spaced 100 metres apart. Between them, they will protrude 25 metres and 17 metres from the gorge rim.

Those who visit the Skywalk will feel as though they're floating on air, while 100 metres above the Murchison River. Spectacular views of the national park are promised for all those who venture to the edge, whether by pram, wheelchair or on foot. These types of enterprise will please some people and upset others. Purists will claim that the wild, untouched beauty is in danger of being tainted. Others will point to the ethical designs of the Skywalk, along with the increased tourism numbers, and the chance to educate more visitors about the importance of the national park.

It might be several years before I return with my family. Maybe next time we'll come at Easter, to enjoy the warm autumnal weather. My first stop will be the feeding station. I'll turn my eyes up to the blue sky and watch the final approach of the first pelican, as it gracefully touches down on the foreshore.

*

[Update] Since writing this chapter the Skywalk has been built, with worldwide acclaim from the hundreds of thousands of visitors to the region each year, including those who have found it reminiscent to the one located in the Grand Canyon, Arizona!

Out of the Blue

"Now, every time I witness a strong person, I want to know: What dark did you conquer in your story? Mountains do not rise without earthquakes."

– Katherine MacKenett

Every summer, thousands of swimmers descend on Australia's southwest to take part in the Busselton Jetty Swim, a 3.6-kilometre, open-water race. The event has grown in stature since its inception in 1996. From humble beginnings and a sign-up of 82 swimmers, mainly from those living locally, it has grown into a blue-ribbon, internationally recognised sporting event.

After returning from Kalbarri, Fran met with her close friend, Rose, to continue with their swim training. This was to be their second year of entry and they were confident about improving their time, especially if the warm spell continued and the wind stayed away. Their plan was to swim side by side during the race, just as before, to support each other along the way.

Two weeks before the big day, with the boys away on a sleepover, I tagged along with Fran one morning. While she chomped on a banana, twiddled with the air conditioning and checked for text messages, I drove through our neighbourhood, noting the household sprinklers trying to bring life to parched gardens. The dashboard temperature display read 25 degrees, and it was just after 6 a.m.

There were already a few parked cars by the beachfront, belonging to dog walkers, joggers and swimmers. From our vantage point, Geographe Bay looked stunning, its turquoise waters stretching towards the horizon. Just offshore, two sea kayaks were in motion, carving through the glassy water towards the main jetty, far to our right. Rose was waiting and greeted us with hugs and a cheery smile. As they prepared for their training swim and chatted excitedly about the upcoming race, I made my way to the beach.

With camera poised, I turned my focus on a cormorant, sunning itself on a wooden post jutting from the ocean. As I snapped away, Fran and Rose passed me by, with promises to return after completing four laps of the net. By now, other swimmers had arrived at the scene. I knew a few by name and recognised familiar faces, each one going through the ritual of kicking off sandals, placing towels away from the water's edge and rinsing goggles before slipping them on.

Just like Fran and Rose, they were soon in the water, swimming close to the protective net. To most locals, the sturdy mesh that drops from the waterline to the seabed is known as the *Shark Net*, but a placard nearby gives it a generic, less dramatic title of *Beach Enclosure,* stretching 450 metres around a series of yellow posts in a protective arc.

The net isn't foolproof, with narrow gaps appearing from time to time when knots fail, or weights get displaced. Days earlier, Fran had returned from a swim, eager to share news about a metre-long gummy shark she'd encountered in the water. Stingrays also find their way into the enclosure, along with schools of fish and nervous crabs! I've seen them on the seabed, beady eyes open, pincers aimed skyward in self-defence as swimmers pass overhead.

On the morning of race day, Fran set the pace to get us out of the door on time. During the drive to the starting line, she chatted away to Noah and Sebastian, ignoring their yawns while asking if they'd take photos during her swim. I drove with the visor down, watching the sun peek over the rooftops. As we approached the foreshore, I glanced towards her and asked, 'So, how are you feeling? Are you nervous?'

She turned the radio down and produced a beaming smile. 'No, I'm really excited. Maybe next year we should enter as a family team of four.'

The idea made me chuckle as I considered such a momentous task. Fran somehow read my mind and set down a challenge. 'I only started swimming with Rose a few years ago and look where we are now. With a few lessons, you could improve your technique.'

'Fran, I haven't got a technique. I just doggy paddle and hope for the best.'

'It's never too late to learn, Ali. You tried surfing in Byron Bay and managed to stand on a board.'

I smiled at the memory and shook my head. 'Fran, I stood for a few seconds, on a gentle wave, close to the beach.'

'It was still a wave, no matter how small. All I'm saying is—'

It was time for me to change the topic, and the sight of our friend, Pascal, walking barefoot down the street, a beach towel draped over wide shoulders, gave me an excuse to call out. I wound the car window down, but he'd darted between snarled traffic and the moment was gone.

Overnight, our tranquil foreshore had been transformed, and I had to hustle for a parking space. Instead of a whisper-quiet vista with just a few early morning swimmers or beachgoers, there were cars and people everywhere. Coffee vans were in demand, as were the flagship cafés that remain open most days of the year, even during the lean winter months. Now, they were enjoying a roaring trade, with queues stretching outside.

As arranged, Fran and Rose met beside one of the majestic fig trees close to shore, unaware of two teenagers above their heads, sitting astride a weeping branch while staring out at sea. The only task left for Fran and Rose was to ensure their arms and legs displayed their race numbers, followed by a dash to the toilets! Once complete, they seemed at ease, chatting freely to other competitors. Nearby, a row of barriers shielded the crowd from the timekeepers and officials.

A loudspeaker announcement hushed the crowd, as an Aboriginal elder welcomed us to country. We soon learned he was from the Wadandi people, the traditional owners of this part of southwest Australia. His voice carried far, acknowledging the land and sea, including the plants and animals that coexist in this wonderful part of the world.

The next broadcast called for the first participants to prepare, signalling a murmur of anticipation as all heads turned towards the beach. A line of men and women stood ready, dressed in swimwear, including gold coloured bathing caps depicting their status as elite swimmers.

With no one else ahead, they'd have the ocean to themselves. Some were local, others from Perth and interstate. A handful had travelled from overseas for the chance to take part and were now moments away from dashing into the water. With luck, one of them would collect the substantial cash prize for breaking the course record.

For Fran and Rose, it wasn't about the chance of a podium finish. Like most others, they were there for the experience and to soak up the atmosphere, while taking on a worthy challenge. Just before they headed to the beach, I guided Fran to one side for a hug. 'Best of luck out there and I'll be watching with the boys. If you want my advice, don't even think about sharks, as it's rare to see them.'

'Why did you have to mention sharks? I haven't thought about them all week. But now you've brought them to my attention and—'

'Fran, look up there. That helicopter's been busy all morning, searching the bay. I've also seen a few drones in action. Don't worry, you'll be fine. I'd be more worried about getting stung by a jellyfish.'

In reply, she gave a smirk and rolled her eyes. 'Oh, thanks. I feel so much better now. Anyway, could you please get a photo of me and Rose?'

They stood together, smiling proudly against a backdrop of sparkling water, white sand and hundreds of other competitors. Some looked calm and composed, chatting with friends or staring out at sea. Others fiddled with goggles or bathing caps while lost in thought.

After wishing them good luck, I called for the boys to follow me to the nearby finger jetty, jutting 30 metres into the ocean. The boardwalk was filled with onlookers, plus a man with a rifle, seated at the end while flanked by a guard. I got close, just as the announcer counted down the last seconds.

To signal the start, the rifleman fired a blank shot into the bright sky. The explosive crack reverberated across the water as the elite swimmers ploughed through the shallows, before taking a dive and starting to swim. Those watching from a distance, clapped, cheered or took photos.

The race organisers then set in motion a series of staggered starts for each batch of swimmers, each with different coloured bathing caps. I waited for the fifth wave, hoping to spot Fran and Rose in the mix. It was Seby that spotted them at the edge of the pack. We watched as they dashed into the water, obscured by arms, bodies and sea spray as those around jockeyed for space.

We caught up with them 20 minutes later. This time we were standing on the main jetty, looking down at the water at hundreds of swimmers. Lifeguards patrolled nearby, some on jet skis, others in kayaks. They were all dressed in red-and-yellow, watching from a safe distance for anyone who might need help or attention. Up above, the helicopter completed another circuit, searching for sharks or signs of distress from swimmers.

As Fran and Rose reached the midway point of the outward leg, I heard a noise from behind me. I turned to find a crowd of onlookers cheering on the leader, now on the other side of the jetty, heading to shore in record time. Like every competitor who took part that day, Fran and Rose received a round of applause at the finishing line.

One of the loudest cheers went to the very last swimmer, a middle-aged woman who made her way to shore, chaperoned by two lifeguards in kayaks. As she approached the beach, a friend stepped towards the shallows, while walking beside a golden Labrador, held firm by a leash. The dog wore a fluorescent vest and stood obediently, its tail wagging as the woman emerged triumphantly from the ocean and carefully stepped onto the sand, her arms outstretched while greeting her dog. She ruffled the dog's head, took hold of the leash and waited for her friend to steer her in the right direction. The dog took over from this point, guiding her across the sand, past the cheering crowd as the event announcer greeted her arrival at the finish line.

Fran and Rose completed the race in a time of one hour and 47 minutes, earning themselves well-deserved hugs and a slap-up breakfast. Partway through, they raised their glasses and made plans to compete in many other sporting events, including fun runs and marathons. The following summer, they borrowed mountain bikes to compete in the X-Adventure, Australia's largest off-road triathlon.

A month after they'd crossed the finish line, our family life was turned upside down, triggered by a routine mammogram and follow-up tests, which confirmed Fran had stage two breast cancer. There was little time to absorb the news as we got swept into a whirlwind, with difficult decisions to make, each with pros and cons. During this time, one thing became clear to me:

So much happened that a book could be written, and one day I hope this comes to fruition, because Fran has a brave and inspiring story to tell.

Plans were put in place for Fran to undergo a double mastectomy, along with immediate reconstruction. The surgery results confirmed the mass was larger than expected, requiring nymph node removal, with recommendations to commence a six-month course of chemotherapy and radiation treatment. Chemotherapy was put on hold when infections set in, caused by problems with the breast reconstruction. The only solution was to have them removed and with chemotherapy a priority, the operation was booked within days.

Throughout this time, just as before, Fran strived to lead a healthy lifestyle–eating the right things–exercising when able–embracing each new day, especially when walking on our local beach with Noah, Sebastian and our dog, Peppi. During these moments, she craved family photos, soaking up the sunshine as well as the laughter and antics while watching our teenage boys run freely along the beach with Peppi.

It was heart-warming to watch her embrace each new day, and in the months that followed she seemed to come to terms with her body shape. It wasn't all good news though, with side effects and niggling pain from the last surgery prompting the need for further advice. A city specialist offered to resolve the problem, along with the opportunity of a natural breast reconstruction using her body fat.

The procedure would take over ten hours, followed by days in hospital and months of rehabilitation. Before the operation, she would need to put on several kilos and after sharing this news with friends, received many generous offers from those who wished to contribute with their own body fat!

Like a bruised and battered fighter, Fran was being asked to go back into the ring. At first, she resisted, although it wasn't just the surgery that caused the hesitation, but also the time away from our two boys. There would be no chance of working for many months and she didn't relish the thought of putting on weight–by eating more–and exercising less–especially after all she'd been through. After much soul searching, she decided to return to the operating table, hoping the specialist could work a double miracle–by removing the problem–as well as creating two new breasts from her body fat.

After waking from the operation, the first thing she noticed was a soft blanket covering her upper body. Not a normal blanket, but one that inflated with a touch of a button, along with temperature sensors and heat pads. Underneath the blanket were more layers, including a sterile dressing protecting her new breasts!

When the specialist completed his daily rounds, I offered him a seat next to Fran's bed. We soon learned there was bittersweet news, as he'd been unable to resolve the original issue despite all efforts. As we absorbed the bad news, he eased out a caring smile and shared the good news. The reconstruction had been a success and Fran now had two new sisters, each one a little different from the other! As this news struck home, Fran sat open-mouthed in tearful amazement, with the realisation she now had new breasts, created naturally.

Her recovery started with sluggish walks along the hospital ward, bent over like a banana while hooked to a mobile drip. After returning home, she continued her daily walks, this time without a drip, taking tentative steps around our neighbourhood streets. With each new day she grew stronger, both physically and mentally, and in the months that followed, there were many hospital visits and during this time we spent time on the road, sometimes for hours, including overnight stays at accommodation provided by the Cancer Council. This gave us the time to reflect on life, including the good times, the hard times, the battles won, and the challenges ahead.

Within six months, her sights were set on a return to work, along with the chance to participate in the Busselton Jetty swim once again. To prepare, she needed extensive physiotherapy to help overcome restricted mobility caused by the reconstruction surgery.

Springtime proved a turning point, with clear skies and calm waters creating a perfect backdrop as she returned to the ocean for the first time in nearly two years! The reunion was heart-warming to watch, as she waded into the ocean–arms out wide–trailing her fingers through the water. Moments later, she took a breath and let the water wash over her body.

In the weeks that followed, she returned to the outdoor pool, gaining confidence with each lap. A pattern soon emerged, meeting Rose by the foreshore each Saturday morning, swimming together alongside the net. During this period, Fran convinced me to take the plunge and sign up for the Busselton Jetty race. Initially, I came up with a list of excuses, including a recurring shoulder injury and work commitments away from home.

She dismissed my complaints with a shrug and a knowing smile. 'There's nothing wrong with your shoulder when you go mountain biking, and you can't work all the time. Besides, the swim will do you good.'

'That's the problem. I can't swim. I've been doing the doggy paddle for 50 years and will never get around the jetty if I swim like a five-year-old.'

She wasn't going to let me off the hook. 'Ali, you're the one who says it's never too late to learn something new. We live near the ocean, and you love the water, so why not learn to swim properly?'

'But the swim is only four months away and I need more time.'

'All you need to do is start the journey! Besides, it's nearly summer, which is a perfect time to learn!'

She then dropped her voice and squeezed my hand. 'Go on, give it a try, just for me. You love a challenge and we'll be out there with Rose and Seby. I'm not sure how I'll go, but will give it my best and enjoy every moment.'

She then picked up a palm-sized calendar we kept by the back door, filled with inspirational quotes. As I watched, she peeled off the *quote of the day* and handed it over. This time it was Helen Keller, an American writer, providing the thoughtful words. She became the first deaf and blind person in the United States to earn a Bachelor of Arts degree. She also travelled to over 35 countries, meeting with world leaders as an advocate to those with vision loss. The quote I read was hard to ignore:

Life is either a daring adventure or nothing.

The combination of Fran's heartfelt request and Helen's stirring words tipped the balance as I came to a decision! The following morning, I was standing waist deep in the clear waters of Geographe Bay, watching Seby glide past while swimming to a nearby buoy. On his return, he removed his goggles and stood close by, his youthful shoulders nearly level with mine. 'See, Dad. That's how you do it. Just keep your face below the water and blow bubbles through your mouth and nose. Then take a breath every third stroke by turning your head and opening your mouth.'

As he continued giving advice, I realised there was so much to think about, including breathing at the right moment, blowing bubbles, arm placement, arm reach, pulling cupped hands through the water, all while kicking in synch and travelling in a straight line!

Before I could ask questions, he gave one more piece of advice, followed by a reality check. 'You'll need to train most days as you've got no technique and are pretty clueless for someone your age.'

'Seby, I grew up in a town that was hours from the North Sea. I only went a few times a year and the water was always cold and murky, even in summer! No one swam for more than a few minutes for fear of frostbite.'

In reply, he reminded me how long I'd been living in Australia, with plenty of time to learn to swim in warmer waters. I nodded in agreement while masking the list of niggling doubts creeping up since agreeing to take part in the swim. I already felt overwhelmed after a late-night stint watching YouTube clips aimed at teaching adult beginners the basics of freestyle. The hipster instructor with thousands of followers had made it look easy, including the chance for further guidance if I subscribed to his newsletter and *liked* his YouTube Channel.

Now I was standing waist deep in the Indian Ocean, watching clouds scurry past, as Seby instructed me to swim to the buoy and back without reverting to the doggy paddle! Not wanting to look like a complainer, I gave him a confident smile while putting on my goggles.

During my first lesson with Seby, I tried my best, but 50 years of doggy paddling had taken their toll. After many false starts, mouthfuls of water and very little distance, I gave up, with a promise to return the following weekend. Despite warmer weather and further encouragement from my teenage instructor, this resulted in similar results.

A week later, I visited the local recreation centre and signed up for swimming lessons with a seasoned instructor. In the calm, clear, chlorinated water, the lessons proved fruitful, with heaps of homework required to put theory into practice, which meant trawling along the outdoor slow lane with other adult beginners. Throughout the next lessons, I picked up the basics of freestyle and swam 25 metres to the delight of my instructor.

Within a few weeks, I completed multiple lengths without stopping, although the instructor requested more time to fix my bizarre technique, which included flailing, uncoordinated legs, and a tendency to swim off course into the lane barrier. I also had difficulty with turning my head to the left, which meant I could only breathe on one side. Not a good technique if waves were breaking from the same direction during race day–as I'd have to revert to the doggy paddle!

With a limited budget and race day approaching, I thanked him for his help and turned my attention to the Busselton foreshore, to swim in the calm waters of Geographe Bay. During my first visit, I felt like an imposter alongside the confident locals, who didn't hesitate as they waded past me towards deeper waters, chatting to friends while adjusting goggles or pointing out schools of fish. In comparison, I stood silently in knee deep water, trying to remember all the things I'd been taught in the previous weeks.

Within a few minutes, I had the foreshore to myself and watched the swimmers head to a yellow post, 100 metres offshore, before taking a turn to the right and following the net. Now it was my turn and with no one around to judge, I took a breath and aimed for the post! After a few strokes, I spluttered and stopped, thankful for the sturdy net which I held onto while catching my breath. I tried again but couldn't get into a rhythm, resulting in more coughs and splutters, followed by a return to the trusted doggy paddle.

Ten minutes had passed, and I'd only made it halfway to the turning point. Once again, I held onto the net while gathering my thoughts. I could turn back to shore, jump in the car and be under a warm shower within fifteen minutes. But if I gave up now, I'd never return and with thoughts of Fran's recent battles, I made a pact to stay in the water until I'd completed a circuit–no matter how long it took. Most of all, I needed to relax–to enjoy the moment–including the school of herring just out of arm's reach!

The fish stayed with me until I reached the first marker and as I held onto the net a handful of swimmers passed by, each one making the task look easy. I then set my sights on the next yellow post and noticed a gull sitting on top. As I approached, the bird stayed put, eyeing me from up high. This stop-start pattern continued for the next hour and during this time I discovered each post acted as a perfect lookout point for resident seabirds.

In the days and weeks that followed, my technique improved, along with my confidence. I was still the slowest swimmer using the nets, but each stop along the circuit gave me the chance to meet and greet the resident bird life. After a time, I began to give each of them a nickname to take my mind off the task ahead.

I usually found Kevin the cormorant on the second post, fanning his wings in the early sunshine. Percy, the pelican, often perched himself high and dry on one of the middle posts or paddled on the other side of the protective net, watching with interest as I swam past.

Three weeks before the race began, I spotted Sammy, the one-legged seagull, hopping on the furthest post, wings poised for take-off as I called out in celebration at achieving the circuit without stopping! While stepping out of the shallows, I realised the jetty swim was eight times longer than the circuit I'd just completed.

By the morning of the race, despite many hours of training, new goggles, and a trimmed stomach, I still felt under prepared for such a feat. Seby, in contrast, looked confident and happy as we stood side by side on the foreshore, surrounded by 2,000 other competitors. This was his third entry into the event, but his first as a solo swimmer and I felt proud to be racing alongside him. Not that we'd see much of each other in the bay, despite his lack of training! Unlike me, he was a natural in the water. At his age, while back in England, I could hardly manage a length of the local pool, let alone an ocean swim.

As I fiddled with my timing chip, Fran came to the rescue and secured it in place around my ankle before turning her attention to the race number that needed to be transferred onto my arm. As she peeled the sticker, I thought it should have been me helping her, after all she'd been through. Soon after, I steered her away from the crowd for a few seconds together.

'Fran, if it wasn't for you, I wouldn't have signed up for the swim. I'm terrified, nervous and excited, all at the same time. I'm proud of your determination to get back into the ocean, where you belong.'

In response, she reached for my hand. 'I'm grateful for lots of things–including your willingness to give it a go and to all those who helped me during my journey. I'm going to take my time and enjoy every moment. Maybe next year, I'll be ready to swim freestyle.'

Just then, a family friend strolled past, looking fit and tanned in lycra swimwear. He stopped to say hello and called out, 'Good luck, Fran. Nice to see you back in the water. We're all cheering for you.'

He then turned his attention to me. 'I didn't know you were a long-distance swimmer, Ali. You kept that one quiet.'

I put on a brave face and said, 'You know me, Paul. A man of many talents.'

After a high five, followed by a 'good luck and see you next week for a beer,' he was gone, and Fran was rummaging around in her daypack. 'Look what I picked up at the chemist. It's locally made and helps against stingers. Now, when you're out there, remember to breathe on both sides or you'll end up crooking your neck.'

While she rubbed cream into my neck, I stared across the waterfront at the thousands of other competitors. Every competitor has a story to tell and it made me wonder how many of them were beginners, just like me, about to swim freestyle for the first time. Maybe some were like Fran–recovering from illness–or maybe they were returning from injury–or attempting a lifelong ambition–and happy to be part of such an iconic event.

As the start time approached, Seby offered a few tips about surviving the dash into the water, where flailing limbs and wayward kicks meant the possibility of having goggles ripped away. He also explained that kicks to the head were possible during the first minutes, with so many people churning through the water. For a few moments, his voice was drowned out by the sound of a helicopter passing overhead, the pilot and crew scanning the water for signs of sharks!

As the drone of the helicopter faded, the event announcer began the countdown. The crowd stirred to life, as each swimmer joined the queue, looking for those with the same coloured bathing caps. Just like Rose, Fran and Seby, I wore a pink cap, depicting the last group of solo swimmers to enter the water.

Just like every year, the event announcer counted down from ten, joined in by the crowd as a rifleman stood ready to pull the trigger. As a shot rang out across the bay, the elite swimmers dashed towards the water, followed at timed intervals by each group.

Those wearing pink caps remained at the back, inching their way to the start line as the sun rose higher. Seby peeled away as the pink caps edged closer to the front, looking for his race line. Fran and Rose had already made a pact to stick together and in the final seconds before reaching the start line, I watched as they edged to the left of the group, hoping for space alongside the jetty.

I stayed at the back, my heart racing at the thought of what lay ahead–not just for me–but also for Fran–knowing she'd soon be surrounded by hundreds of swimmers–hoping she'd stay out of trouble, away from the churn. I then searched for a friendly face in the crowd that lined the jetty. But there were too many people and I needed to concentrate on the task ahead.

I then heard the blast from an air horn and suddenly I was racing towards the water, all thoughts of a game plan forgotten. To my left, the crowd cheered as each swimmer ran into the shallows, some tripping or faltering in their haste to get into deeper water. Moments later, I was waist deep and those around me were charging ahead, duck diving into the water and getting into a rhythm. I followed suit, just as a wayward swimmer cut across me–or was I cutting across her? Then there were more bodies, close enough to brush past me as they overtook with each confident stroke.

Another swimmer appeared by my side, maybe a man or woman–it was hard to know amid the froth and noise. Whether male or female, they had powerful legs and knocked off my googles with a swinging foot. I'd only been in the water for 30 seconds and needed to tread water while attempting to reposition my goggles.

Before setting off again, I took the time to study the scene. There were a few stragglers close by, and one or two that looked as flustered as me, adjusting goggles or converting to breaststroke. But we were few, compared to the many that were now heading out to sea, their pink caps bobbing in the water.

The winner that day was 19-year-old Kyle Lee, in a record-breaking time of 38 minutes, 59 seconds. While he was collecting his winner's medal, I was still on the outward leg. By the time I reached the halfway mark, the wind had picked up and most swimmers were out of sight. For a while, I treaded water close to the timber pylons at the end of the jetty, trying to catch my breath as feisty waves broke around me. Most spectators had vanished, as those they were following had already crossed the finish line. While I pondered my next move, a lifeguard on a bright yellow board paddled nearer and called out to me. 'Well done, mate. You're halfway there!'

I gave her the thumbs up and turned to face the beach, nearly two kilometres away. I then set off, with the jetty to my left, hoping to keep it in sight while taking a breath between strokes. Within a hundred metres, I began to falter, with sharp pains across my neck each time I turned my head to the left. The only way to keep moving was to revert to the slow and steady doggy paddle or continue with freestyle while taking a breath to my right after every third stroke. I chose the speedier option without realising the wind and current was pulling me off course.

With each laboured breath, I searched for a marker or buoy to guide me and spotted a lifeguard close by, keeping her distance as I ploughed through the water. Minutes later she paddled closer, just as the spotter helicopter began circling.

She must have noticed my shocked expression and called out above the sound of the engine and swishing blades. 'No need to worry, mate. We're just wondering where you're going, as you seem to be heading to Dunsborough instead of the finish line.'

I peeled off my fogged goggles and looked around, noticing how far I'd swam away from the jetty. By now, her board was close enough to touch as she bobbed on the water while offering help. 'If you hold on, I'll paddle you back to the jetty.'

At that moment, I could have said yes to her offer. After all, it was just a nudge towards the jetty to resume the race. I also considered bailing out altogether. With aching limbs and a belly of saltwater, the thought of a free ride to shore on a powerful jet ski proved hard to ignore. Then I thought of Fran, taking on the challenge despite many hurdles and heartbreak. If she could do it, so could I and with this thought I called out to the lifeguard. 'I'm okay, thanks. I'll keep going as long as I can.'

She smiled and said, 'No worries, mate. You're doing great. I'll keep out of your way, but will be here if you need me.'

As if to reassure me, she then pointed towards the circling helicopter. 'Don't worry about sharks. The only thing they've spotted so far is a friendly dolphin.'

I gave her a wave and set off once more, listening to the growl of the helicopter as it flew overhead. In the silence that followed, I found a rhythm while watching for signs of sea life below. A school of silvery fish held my attention for a few seconds, followed by the sight of a blue manna crab emerging from a patch of seagrass, its powerful pincers thankfully out of reach. Further on, I spotted timber pylons scattered across the sandy seabed and wondered if they were a relic from days long gone when the jetty had been pounded by a cyclone.

With each weary stroke and kick of the legs, I inched my way to the finish line, drawing strength from all the times that Fran had dug deep during her battles. As the wind picked up, I heard the event announcer's voice, booming from loudspeakers. I had no idea of the words being spoken but was aware there was a cut-off time and maybe they were packing away!

As I stopped for rest, the lifeguard paddled into view and called out a few words of support. 'Keep going, mate! You've nearly done it. What a legend!'

Spurred on by her praise, I kicked hard for the beach, determined to enjoy the last few moments in the water. Seconds after stepping ashore on that warm summer's morning, Fran rushed to my side, smiling and clapping as we hugged by the shoreline. She'd also finished the race and had a colourful towel as a memento, handed out to each competitor as they crossed the line.

Seby appeared on the scene, looking bright eyed and energetic after finishing an hour earlier, his finisher's towel wrapped casually around his slim waist. After I punched the air in delight, he gave me a high five, followed by the words I longed to hear. 'Well done, Dad. You did alright!'

Although the crowd had thinned, there were still hundreds on the beach, their claps and cheers warming my heart as I watched a group of volunteers race onto the beach to remove event banners and flags. The finish line by the water's edge was quickly dismantled, prompting me to head towards the event announcer, calling out my name.

Fran ran alongside me as I crossed the line in a time of 2 hours, 50 minutes! I'd come last by a long way but didn't care in the slightest. Instead, I savoured every moment, feeling the warmth of the crowd as the adrenaline took over. Like an Olympic athlete achieving gold, I held my hands high as the official photographer snapped his last shot of the day. I was so glad to have competed in such an iconic event, along with Fran, Seby and Rose. Moments later, I received a handshake and a finisher's towel, depicting the famous jetty and a lone swimmer.

The ending of the Busselton Jetty swim helps bring this book to its natural conclusion. The stories within these pages are in sequential order and span many years. As I write this passage from a local café, I'm glad to report that Fran is still an avid swimmer, along with Rose, of course! She can swim freestyle again and is also back into running, especially during weekend mornings, striding side by side with Rose along the length of the jetty. Sometimes they spot dolphins in the bay or get the chance to call out to anglers as they cast their lines from the wooden railings into the calm waters, far below.

Our boys have grown fast, and Noah has recently flown the nest. After travelling across the east coast of Australia with his cousin Angus and a group of friends, they now have southeast Asia in their sights! Seby is still involved in sports and is a natural in the kitchen, as well as the ocean. He also has plans to travel far and wide and has recently passed his driving test! Just like my dad, the merchant sailor who left his native Scotland to travel the world, it seems that Noah and Seby have inherited a taste for the open road.

During Fran's recovery, we sold the camper trailer to a friend, with instructions on how to connect the poles and pull out the canvas. We then purchased a pop-top caravan, with bold plans to venture around parts of Australia once more. It seems a long time ago we went in search of long-necked turtles in Kakadu, with Patsy, the Aboriginal guide. Time has flown quickly since we arrived in Australia, with many dreams and aspirations. We were only going to stay for a year or two, but there seems to be so much more to explore, making sure to enjoy the journey as well as the destination.

We still miss our family, friends and the countryside of Britain and Ireland, but Australia is our home now. On summer evenings we sit by our front porch, binoculars poised for the chance to spot kangaroos in the adjacent wetlands. The Indian Ocean is just a cycle ride away and we even have a local beachside bar and restaurant, offering the chance of happy hour drinks every Friday evening!

If you're ever by the foreshore in Busselton during spring and summer, you might see us with other locals, either in a beachside café or cycling with friends. If the weather is kind, you might spot Fran in the ocean, while the boys take turns jumping from the jetty. I'll be close to the marine net, practising my freestyle while looking out for blue manna crabs or schools of fish, feeling thankful for making the move Down Under all those years ago.

Finding my Voice

"If you have the words, there's always a chance that you'll find the way."

– Seamus Heaney

With three brothers, one sister and a crazy dog called Barney, there was rarely a dull moment in my childhood home. We grew up in a three-bedroom rental which overlooked an expanse of trampled grass frequented by dog walkers and boisterous kids, playing football each weekend while using jumpers as goalposts.

This additional story is about my older brother, Michael. He was the kind of person who always left an impression and in the following passage you'll learn about the positive impact he had on me–especially during my teenage years. We lived in the multicultural town of Luton, 30 miles north of London. Each year, the town attracts millions of visitors, drawn to the international airport for budget flights to warmer climes.

Each summer, Mum and Dad would drive us across England and Wales, to board a ferry for Ireland, before travelling north and west to County Donegal, renowned for its misty hills and wild coastline, with a different beach for each day of the year! The welcoming pubs offer traditional music and the landscape inspires poets, painters and songwriters to capture the raw beauty of this *secret* corner of Ireland.

Throughout the long journey Michael would keep us entertained, with jokes to tell or wry observations as Mum struggled with map reading and Dad muttered at the wheel. For two weeks, we'd stay with my grandmother in the two-storey house where she once raised 15 children. Painted a dazzling white and set upon the side of a lush hill, it was impossible to miss from the undulating road that cut through the valley. During each holiday, I felt wild and free, surrounded by hills and sheep.

Dad's car was always in demand, either to take Gran to town or to ferry excited children on day trips, including fishing ports, mountain trails and bustling villages. On special evenings, I'd sit with a fizzy drink in one of the local pubs, listening to tales from long ago as my great uncles, Barney and Francie, enthralled visitors with their recitations of life in rural Donegal. Each of them was a Seanchaí–an Irish storyteller–and I soon became convinced that Michael had inherited their gift.

While home in England, I spent many teenage nights staring from my bedroom window at the lights of the airport tower, daydreaming about travelling far and wide. But as the years flew by, insecurity and shyness held me back–until Michael intervened, becoming my mentor and life coach! Being a few years older and somewhat bolder, he'd venture to London for weeks on end, returning with tall tales while handing out trinkets, vinyl records and outlandish clothes not yet for sale in our hometown.

As I matured, the bright lights beckoned, and Michael played a part in helping me to find my voice and identity. Being out with him on a Saturday night was like strutting alongside a celebrity as we graced each high street pub. Everyone knew him and he'd often disappear into the crowd, drawn to a dancefloor or pulled towards a table of raucous patrons, eager to hear one of his colourful stories.

Sometimes we'd return home together–to talk about travel–and music–and meaningful lyrics, sitting together in our cramped bedroom while listening to the words of Lennon, McCartney, Dylan and Springsteen. For years, we played football together in a local team and although he had an abundance of skills, he got the most pleasure while making our teammates laugh, rather than showing off his fancy footwork.

Years flew by and Michael remained the same. He enjoyed being the joker and always looked out for the needy–including me. He never discriminated or judged and had a wide range of friends, from young to old and black to white, including the rich and poor. He was usually the last to leave a party and always the one to help newcomers feel at home. Those who *really* knew him didn't just see the comedian, but also the deep thinker with a sense of curiosity, who'd just as easily bypass a pub in search of a city museum. With each new year, the antics mellowed, but his zest for life rarely wavered, nor his ability to make people smile each day.

While in our thirties, we both married and within a few years Michael moved away from England to set up home with his wife, Maureen, and their two children, in County Donegal, Ireland. The heritage town of Ardara always had a special place in his heart, ever since our childhood holidays staying with Gran. He made plans to start a business while giving his children, Becky and Louie, the space and time to grow in a rural setting, surrounded by relatives.

I also made a move from our hometown. When General Motors unexpectedly announced the closure of the nearby car factory, I took my chance and headed overseas with my wife, Fran. We first ventured to South America, then Africa, before settling in Western Australia.

We've been here 20 years and during this time have raised a family of our own, with our two boys, Noah and Sebastian, looking to travel far and wide in the years ahead. We enjoy getting visitors from back home and return to England and Ireland every three to four years for summer holidays. One sadness is that Michael never visited us in Australia, either due to business ventures, family commitments and in later years, a fight for his life against throat cancer. He overcame the first battle fifteen years ago but bore the scars with a butchered neck because of complex, but necessary, surgery.

A few years ago, he collapsed during an overseas business trip and within days we'd heard the cancer had returned. This time, the doctors were not so optimistic. Upon hearing the news, I felt torn between two sides of the world, as Fran had recently undergone a number of operations due to breast cancer and was about to begin chemotherapy and radiation treatment. During her recovery from another operation, I received news from Ireland that Michael was looking forward to seeing me and within hours I'd booked my flight.

After a teary farewell from Fran's hospital bed, I flew 9,000 miles to meet Michael and his family. He greeted me with a soft hug and over the following days, whenever he had the strength, I sat close by while he scribbled words onto paper, his once dulcet tones reduced to a croaky and painful rasp from the aggressive tumour that could not be contained. When the time came to head back to Australia, there were tears and promises to meet again, as we stood by his doorway to admire the Atlantic waters creeping into the bay, perfectly framed by green hills and faraway mountains.

A day later I touched down in Western Australia, then drove three hours south to meet Fran and the children. I'd missed her first chemotherapy treatment by 24 hours and sat by her side as she recounted each moment, including the support from Jan, our neighbour, who'd offered to help while I'd been away.

I soon learned about the warmth of the nurses and the sting of the needle, followed by tea and scones while she was hooked to a drip. Afterwards, instead of returning home with Jan, she found the mental strength to run four kilometres around an adjacent park, as prescribed by a specialist from Edith Cowan University. Their research has shown that exercise might be a key weapon in the battle against cancer and Fran had embraced each piece of professional advice.

Soon after, the topic turned to Michael, with Fran and the boys sitting quietly as I shared news about his fighting spirit despite the battle he faced. Sometime later, to brighten the mood, I handed out gifts, with ill-fitting Donegal T-shirts telling me the boys were growing fast and a handwoven jumper for Fran, made from Irish wool and a perfect fit!

In the months that followed, we stayed in touch with Michael via text messages and video calls. While Fran underwent further surgery and began to recover, Michael's condition slowly deteriorated, but we remained in contact most days. During each video call, he'd appear on our screen, masking his discomfort with a weary smile, holding a pen or marker to scribble a few words of encouragement for Fran. These special moments are etched into our memories, with Fran drawing strength and inspiration from his wise words, despite his struggles and pain.

When he died, my friends in Australia tried saying the right thing. Despite their kind words, I felt irked rather than comforted, mainly because they'd never been able to meet him and couldn't truly contemplate my loss. A few months passed and one evening I sat on my porch, reminiscing to Fran about my childhood, including the colourful characters that had shaped my early life.

As I recited each comical tale, Michael's name continually cropped up. The more Fran laughed, the more I recounted long forgotten moments. Days later, fuelled by her enthusiasm I decided to write a stand-up Fringe show–so that my friends–and anyone else that dared to buy a ticket–would discover a little more about my time with Michael, including the antics in our childhood street. On reflection, without realising it, the telling of stories was my way of healing and during this period, nothing else seemed to matter.

After a nudge from Fran, I called the director of the Fringe to explain the concept of the show and to my surprise got the thumbs up. He then explained I had ten weeks to prepare and would perform at one of Busselton's oldest buildings–The Weld Theatre–built in 1881. With a licensed bar, 120 seats, stage lighting and a rehearsal room, it would be the perfect location. All I needed to do was write the script, find some actors, build numerous props, begin rehearsals, and try selling tickets, all while working full time, mainly away from home! During this time, I came up with a name and tagline for the show:

Soundtrack: A one hour show, filled with rock, pop and classic tunes, including bite-sized stories brought to life with a sprinkle of drama.

Over the following weeks, the rehearsals went well, as each young actor learned their lines, reciting tales about the friendly folk from my childhood streets. As for ticket sales, I'd pledged half the profits to two charities that had helped Fran and Michael during their cancer journeys. With two weeks to go, we'd sold ten tickets. With a week to go, we'd sold 35. Then, without rhyme or reason, the day before the show I got an email from the Fringe director: "*Congratulations, your show is a sell-out.*"

The next line read: "*Please be aware that Soundtrack is the first show of the Fringe Festival–which means the Mayor of Busselton will be there to open it.*"

On the evening of the show, minutes before the heavy curtains drew back, I peeked through a gap to watch the mayor greet the packed house. I recognised some friends within the crowd but there were also many unknown faces–who'd paid good money to be entertained! After thanking the guests for supporting the festival, he then called out that he was looking forward to watching the comedy show–called Soundtrack!

As the theatre hushed and the lights dimmed, my legs turned to jelly. There had to be a mistake! Had all these people come to watch a comedy show? Although there has only ever been one comedian in my family, I felt at that moment

Michael was by my side, urging me to find my voice–just like our great uncles, Barney and Francie, all those years ago.

Seconds before walking on stage I took a breath and caught my reflection in a nearby mirror. I gave myself a thumbs up before smiling at the youthful actors waiting in the wings, ready to re-enact parts of Michael's life. The crowd would soon learn of his childhood in Luton, his antics in London and passion for music. They'd also see a sketch about the time he built a giant music speaker, along with his close friend, Brian. Once complete, they opened a bedroom window, put on a vinyl record and blasted out a song.

At the same time, three streets away, our mum got off her bus, loaded down with shopping, along with many other neighbours. Each of them heard the iconic sound of The Clash belting over the rooftops and most knew the direction it was coming from! Mum took it all in her stride, and by the time she turned the corner, Michael was by her side, eager to carry her bags as the words to *London Calling* resounded across the suburbs.

The show was met with acclaim and the young, inexperienced actors, did themselves proud. My youngest boy, Seby, played the part of Michael and rose to the occasion, complete with a cheeky smile and impromptu acting that was not in the script! As the show came to an end, some audience members were dancing in the aisles to a Springsteen classic, while others clapped and cheered. For an hour in Western Australia, Michael had come to town–and as he always did–he left those he'd met with a smile on their face and a spring in their step!

After the show, I received hugs and handshakes, with appeals to perform another one the following week. I felt drained but happy, with a newfound confidence to tell more inspirational stories, just like Michael used to, after we'd been shown the way by our great uncles, Barney and Francie, all those years ago in the wilds of Donegal.

Acknowledgements

Without Fran's guidance and help, these stories would still be scribbles on a page, rather than words in a book. Time and time again, she encouraged me to fulfil my passion. Within a few of these stories, I have occasionally changed the names of the people involved.

I also mention Michael, one of my brothers. Sadly, he passed away a few weeks after reading the final draft of the chicken story, giving me the nod of approval via a video call. His passing has left a void that will never be filled. During his last hours, with his family by his side, he wrote the following words: *We could all do with a little less stress.*

These stories are dedicated to Michael and our sister, Alice. She planned to travel to Australia to help support Fran during her pregnancy with Sebastian, but was involved in a tragic accident weeks before. Both are missed beyond words. Alice was a quiet warrior with a gentle soul, always eager to help. Michael pushed the boundaries, forming friendships across the world with his wit, charm and wisdom. I so wish he'd written more!

Thanks also to the following local cafés, coffee shops and bars who have supplied nibbles and drinks while I've been tapping away on my laptop during weekends or early mornings over many years.

Brewalicious
The Good Egg
Tonic by the Bay
Shelter Brewing Co
The Goose Beach Bar
The Urban Coffee House

I enjoy keeping in touch with readers and you can find me at the following locations:

On my website @ alistairmcguinness.com
On Facebook @ alistairmcguinnesswriter
On Instagram @ alistair_mcguinness

I've started a Podcast, called *A Taste of Australia*, where I get the chance to chat with travel enthusiasts who have a story to tell about their journeys in Australia. Come pay a visit sometime, or maybe consider being a guest–while telling your own travel stories about Australia.

Happy travels,
Alistair

A Taste of Australia:

Bite-Sized Travels Across a Sunburned Country

"Alone and afraid, I shook my head in astonishment and tried to sum up the situation. This had to be the most dangerous tourist attraction in Australia, yet there were no disclaimer forms to fill in–no friendly guides to offer advice–no ropes to hold on to–and no adrenaline junkies waiting in line. It was just me–halfway up the tallest climbing tree in the world–holding on for dear life!"

Renowned for its ice-cold beers, endless summers, deadly creatures and friendly locals, Alistair was keen to discover the people and places that make Australia one of the most popular travel destinations in the world. These escapades have taken him to the top of Sydney Harbour Bridge and into the searing outback, foraging for bushtucker with an Aboriginal guide.

Along the way, he's experienced the boom and bust of Kalgoorlie, where heat and dust are a way of life and everyone in town knows the price of gold. From the wilds of Tasmania to the bustling laneways of Melbourne and laid-back vibe of Perth, join Alistair as he goes in search of the *real* Australia, from deserts to the ocean, including the island of Rottnest for the chance to meet the cutest creature on planet earth.

Postcards from South America:

A Pig in a Taxi, Cotopaxi and Two Sticks of Dynamite

After losing his job, Alistair takes the plunge and travels into the wilds of South America with his wife. Months later, they were running for their lives in Bolivia!

Join Alistair and Fran as they raft down the Amazon, teach English in the jungle, climb volcanoes and endure a hair-raising taxi ride across the Andes, along with a pig! Before tackling the Inca trail, they hired a donkey called Angus and trekked across a remote mountain pass, with just a mud map to guide them.

While venturing off the beaten track, they discovered Inca ruins, bustling markets and mountain villages inhabited by kindly folk offering food and shelter. If you enjoy fun-filled travel stories, *Postcards from South America* will tempt you to reach for a map, pack your bags and take the trip you've always dreamed about!

Wild About Africa:

Sleepwalking on Kilimanjaro and Running from Lions

Take a seat up front on an overland truck for the best view of Africa, during a journey from Kilimanjaro to Cape Town. During Alistair's first week, he came face to face with a marauding hyena. It didn't help that he was barefoot, in boxer shorts and a T-shirt, while in the wilds of the Serengeti. Soon after, he was robbed of all his possessions.

Luckily, he loaned a pair of pink tracksuit pants and a baggy Arran jumper, to wear while climbing Kilimanjaro, the highest freestanding mountain in the world. If you've ever wondered what it's like to drive across the Ngorongoro Crater on a dawn safari, touch the snows of Kilimanjaro, go quad biking across the Namib Desert or visit the prison that once held Nelson Mandela, this fun packed story is just the ticket for an inspirational adventure.

End to End:

John O'Groats, Broken Spokes and a Dog called Gretna

When three friends set off on a 900-mile trip to explore Britain, using an out of date map to guide them, the scene is set for a wayward adventure. One cyclist didn't own a bike, but luckily, his brother was working out of town and had one in his garage. Painted racing green, with wide wheels and a robust frame, it was far from perfect for such a trip. But it was free!

Along the way they visited numerous country pubs, went in search of the remaining Beatles, discovered an ancient hideaway used by Scottish clans, and survived a storm in the Highlands. Each time they got lost they were helped by a variety of kind and quirky characters.

If you like adventure travel books, then you'll enjoy this tale about three ordinary men, proving that extraordinary things can happen, just when you least expect it. For one of the cyclists, the journey would change his life forever.

Slow Down and Enjoy the Ride

Is it possible to cycle 1,000 miles across Britain in 13 days and still find the time to slow down and enjoy the ride? Twenty years after riding from Land's End to John O'Groats, Alistair set out with his friends to repeat the adventure and quickly discovered that times have changed. Bike computers have replaced maps and thousands of cycle paths now criss-cross Britain. It didn't help that he now lives in Australia and spends more time on a paddleboard than two wheels.

With little training and a borrowed bike, he set off from Land's End, determined to enjoy every moment. Faced with so many natural distractions, he soon began deviating from the plan. With many miles to cover along remote tracks, these diversions came at a price and something had to break. Would it be the bike, the camaraderie or Alistair's inquisitive nature?

Along the way he survived heatstroke in Devon, went in search of a lady called Daphne, and braved wild storms in Glasgow. After a swim in Loch Ness, he found time to enjoy a beer in one of the remotest pubs in Scotland. Everyone who travels across Britain has a story to tell. This is Alistair's.

If you like travel books, you'll enjoy this inspirational story, which shows that with luck, curiosity and perseverance, anything is possible.

Printed in Great Britain
by Amazon

40855733R00155